Ethnic Conflict in California History

Letters and Science Extension Series
University of California, Berkeley

Great Men of Physics: The Humanistic Element in Scientific Work

Ethnic Conflict in California History

A Century of Scientific Discovery

Tinnon-Brown, Inc., *Book Publishers*
10835 Santa Monica Boulevard
Los Angeles, California 90025

ETHNIC CONFLICT

IN CALIFORNIA HISTORY

Woodrow W. Borah

Sherburne F. Cook

Moses Rischin

Stanford M. Lyman

John Modell

Velesta Jenkins

Charles Wollenberg

Mervyn M. Dymally

Samuel Ortega

Edited by

Charles Wollenberg

SBN Number: 87252-021-8
LC Number: 71-101518

Cover Design by Neal Hancock

Introduction

This volume is an exercise in historical muckraking. To a greater or lesser degree, each of our authors has challenged the popular interpretation of California's past, which emphasizes only the romantic and the colorful, only the positive and the progressive. Most of our chapters dwell upon one of California's most sordid traditions: the long heritage of racial prejudice, discrimination, and oppression.

The book has evolved from a public lecture series sponsored by the University of California Extension Division in the summer of 1968. I coordinated the program with considerable help from Judith Johnson and Marvin Chachere of the Extension staff. The public response was far greater than we expected, and because of this we decided to publish the lectures in book form. The lecturers have been kind enough to rewrite or edit the tape-recorded transcripts of their talks, and in some cases they have decided to include the text of the questions and answers which followed the formal presentations.

It should be emphasized that the lectures were intended for a general audience rather than a group of specialists; thus, some of the material included in this book already is well known to scholars in the field. Also, limitations of time and personnel did not allow us to cover the entire subject of ethnic conflict in California history. The book does fill at least two of the subject-matter gaps in the lecture series by including Velesta Jenkins' essay on black Californians and John Modell's essay on the Japanese, which were not part of the original program.

Introduction

A common theme which runs through many of our chapters is the oppressive treatment of non-white people by white people in California history. Most of our authors have produced historical case-studies of what the Kerner Commission called "white racism in America." It probably is significant that none of the authors bothered to make a distinction between "racial conflict" and "ethnic conflict," and none of them mentioned the considerable discrimination suffered by white European immigrants at various times in California history. Perhaps a future generation of historians will consider this emphasis on "white racism" to be excessive, and will criticize some of our authors for being content to describe the effects of ethnic conflict rather than analyzing its causes.

But this book is a product of our times; the lectures contained herein were delivered during a summer of assassination and violence. At one point during the program we were forced to vacate the lecture hall early because a curfew had been placed on the city of Berkeley. As our country has become increasingly aware of racial injustice and increasingly immersed in social discord, it is hardly surprising that historians have been drawn to a study of racial conflict in the past. They simply are following the dictum that "each generation must write its own history," that the perspectives, problems, and even the terminology of the present inevitably affect the questions historians ask of the past.

I believe that the historians who contributed to this book have asked good questions and thus have used the past to contribute to an understanding of the present. In the process they have challenged some of the comfortable assumptions many of us have had about our history. Perhaps this is best illustrated by a question posed by a young schoolteacher in the audience during the lecture series. She was disturbed by the fact that interpretations contained in the lectures conflicted with those in the textbook she was using in her class. "What should we teach?" she asked. The answer, of course, is that we should teach as much of the whole truth about the past as we can. And the horizon of that truth is widened only if we are willing to ask new questions of the past, only if we are willing not to take our history for granted. It is in this spirit that this book is written.

Charles Wollenberg

Berkeley, California
   August, 1969

Contents

Chapter I

The California Mission

Woodrow W. Borah

Juan Rodriquez Cabrillo's "discovery" of California in 1542
came at least 30,000 to 50,000 years after man had first arrived in
the region. When Spain finally settled the California coast in 1769,
there was a population of perhaps 300,000 Indians within the
borders of the present-day state. Thus, the establishment of Spanish settlements was, in part, a process of conquest. The coastal
Indians were deprived of their native territories and brought under
the white man's control. Indian culture and society were trans-
formed to meet the needs of the Spanish empire.

The chief Spanish institution in this colonial effort was the
mission, described in this chapter by Dr. Woodrow W. Borah. Dr.
Borah emphasizes the mission's political and economic role, for
not only were the Indians to be Christianized, they were also to be
made into useful members of a European society. Dr. Borah is
Professor of History at the University of California, Berkeley. He
is a specialist in Spanish American colonial history and is the
author of many articles and monographs including *America as
Model: The Demographic Impact of European Expansion Upon
the Non-European World,* and *New Spain's Century of Depression.*

The California Mission

Between 1769 and 1846, missionaries, soldiers, and settlers from Mexico brought the California Indians into touch with Hispanic culture. Many Indians were brought directly under Hispanic control. The chief instrument of this extension of Hispanic culture was the mission—hence the name given to this lecture; but working with the missions, and sometimes against them, were soldiers and settlers, a civil population with another policy, related to the missions but distinct from them. Politically the years of Hispanic domination of California must be divided into two subperiods: From 1769 to 1821, California, with Mexico, was part of the Spanish dominions, and the missions were the mainstay of royal policy in bringing and keeping the northern outposts within the realms of Spain. From 1821 to 1846, California was part of an independent Mexico which secularized the missions and favored the civil population. Each of the two periods, then, showed a somewhat different policy in the treatment of the California Indians and a somewhat different conception of their place in Hispanic society.

The Indian population of California in 1769 has been estimated at from 125,000 to 300,000. On the whole, the higher estimate seems the better. It would average out to under two persons per square mile in the 160,000 square miles of our state. The Indians were divided into numerous small groups, most of them speaking different languages, and each with its own leaders and own customs. Implements were of stone, wood, and bone. Agriculture was unknown, but the rich resources of the state yielded food through hunting, fishing, and gathering. Acorns from the many California oaks yielded a substitute for grain; the acorns

[3]

were gathered, ground into meal, the meal washed to remove the tannic acid, and then cooked into mush or baked into flat cakes like the Mexican tortilla. The California Indians were a peaceful population, in which crime or insult might be avenged by blood feud but in which groups seldom warred on other groups. In 1775–1776, a Franciscan missionary, Father Francisco Garcés, traveled from the Yuma crossing of the Colorado through much of southern California and the central valley; he passed from Indian group to Indian group without molestation, everywhere received with much kindness.

The people who brought Hispanic culture to California were mostly Mexicans rather than Spaniards born in Spain. They had behind them the centuries of Spanish conquest and the development in Mexico of a country of Hispanic culture. In that process, Indian states of advanced culture with strongly developed classes of peasants, artisans, merchants, nobility, priests, and rulers had been taken over by the Spaniards. The incoming Europeans replaced the topmost groups with a new ruling class, a new nobility, a new priesthood, and increasingly new middle classes, but always left a place for the Indians, who became the source of labor and supplies. Through centuries of living in the same region and interbreeding, more often without benefit of marriage, new mixed racial groups came into being. To them black Africans contributed substantially, for the Spaniards imported numbers of slaves, whom they used as foremen and auxiliaries in their dealings with the Indians. The Negroes tended to disappear rather rapidly into the surrounding population; today there are almost no traces in Mexico of the tens of thousands who came. In the eighteenth century, the subjects of the King of Spain who came to California from Mexico ranged from Spaniards born in Spain or in Mexico to racial mixtures that included much Mexican Indian and Negro. None came to be part of a lower class. The lowest soldiers planned or hoped to receive service and support from the Indians in the new lands.

Prior to 1769 there had been brief, sporadic contacts between the California Indians and the Spaniards. At long intervals, from the time of Cortés, the Spaniards had sent exploring ships along the coast of California. The name Cape Mendocino commemorates one sent out by Antonio de Mendoza, first Viceroy of Mexico and bitter rival of Cortés. Landing parties sent out from the exploring vessels made some contact with the natives. The Manila galleons, coasting down the California shore on their long journeys back from the Philippines, probably made similar brief contacts when they sent parties ashore for fresh water. One galleon, commanded by Cermeño, was wrecked on the northern California coast, and provided the natives with Chinese wares. It was, however, an English party, that of Sir Francis Drake, which probably had the longest contact with California Indians in a five weeks' sojourn on the northern California coast at Drake's Bay or somewhere nearby. But none of these parties had any lasting influence that can be detected, or penetrated far inland. The one exception to this statement is that the Europeans may have brought diseases that spread through the natives far beyond the point of contact. Aside from that possibility, the California Indians in 1769 remained much as they had been two centuries earlier except for changes initiated among themselves.

What brought the Spanish into California was not the beauty or the resources of the region but events outside it. The Russians, exploring across Siberia, crossed the Bering Strait into Alaska and began to send ships down the coast of North America. The British, who had been the most effective rivals of the Spanish in the Atlantic Ocean, were also beginning to show interest in the Pacific coasts and islands. Perhaps the major reason that the Spanish monarchy decided to move into California, therefore, was to ward off a possible threat to Mexico and to the Spanish possessions in the Pacific by extending a chain of forts far to the north. Another reason, although a lesser one, was that the Spanish in the eighteenth century were having serious trouble with the Indians of what is today northern Mexico and our Southwest. In that area, during the late sixteenth and seventeenth centuries, there developed a resurgent Indian culture, an effective Indian response to European challenge, in which the Indians adopted many

European customs and items of European technology, particularly the horse and the gun. They developed a new organization and new tactics of warfare that made them formidable adversaries from perhaps 1690 until the 1890's. For two centuries the frontier in northern Mexico was continually harried by a reorganized Indian society, the Apaches and Comanches being the best-known groups. During much of this time the Indians at the least were a match, and often more than a match, for the men of Hispanic culture. A further motive for the Spanish advance into California, then, was to establish bases behind the Indians of the northern Mexican frontier so that the Spanish, if need arose, could press upon them from yet another side.

The Spanish advance into California was also bound up with a far-reaching reorganization of the Spanish empire that took place after 1763. Spain had received a swift and humiliating defeat from the British when it entered the Seven Years' War on the side of the French. Charles III, the greatest king of the reforming Bourbon dynasty in Spain, determined to reorganize his realms and set about solving many problems. It was one of Charles' most trusted agents, José de Gálvez, later Minister for the Indies, who came to Mexico for a long inspection and recommended occupation of California. He was also largely responsible for the large-scale reorganization of the northern Mexican provinces into a new military command called the Commandancy-General of the Interior Provinces. The new centralized military command in the north at least was able to contain Indian marauders and bring a period of relative peace to the frontier. California became part of the territory of the new military command.

Spanish plans for the occupation of California, as formulated by José de Gálvez, set the policy for the first subperiod, 1769–1821. The royal government never contemplated a mass transfer of population to California. What it aimed at was sending in a relatively small number of soldiers and missionaries and a few settlers to man a limited number of fortified or semifortified points, some of them presidios or forts, some of them towns, to hold down the country. The soldiers and settlers sent from Mexico fundamentally constituted garrisons. There was no intention of driving out the Indians or destroying them. Rather they were to become part of a new social structure as the lower class, furnishing labor and services to the people from Mexico, but also living in their own settlements under the guidance of Christian missionaries. They were to be grouped into more compact settlements or pueblos and were to be taught to be good Christians and industrious peasants and workers. What was planned was very much like the process that had taken place in Mexico, where substantial Indian populations had been harnessed to Hispanic purposes and had been fused in the end into Hispanic society.

The main instrumentality for the Spanish policy was the mission. The term had acquired a very special meaning in Spanish usage. Over a period of more than two centuries, the Spanish in America had worked out a theory of the mission as an instrument for handling Indians and harnessing aboriginal societies to the Spanish state. Certain religious orders—the Franciscans, Dominicans, and Jesuits—were especially active in developing missions in Mexico in the sixteenth and seventeenth centuries, in New Mexico in the seventeenth and eighteenth centuries, and elsewhere in Spanish America. The Jesuit missions in Paraguay were perhaps the best-known instance of the use of missions. Almost an entire country was controlled through religious missions, with the Spanish settlements confined to a small part of the area.

The establishment of missions always meant that members of a religious order were sent to persuade the Indians to settle around churches in organized communities, with central buildings, storehouses, communal fields and pastures, and with the entire population held under careful supervision by the missionaries for religious instruction, work, recreation, and indeed all community and personal life. That kind of communal life and acceptance of rigid discipline, however benevolent the intentions behind it, could be brought about only by coercion, and that in turn meant that soldiers must be near the missionaries, for the missionaries alone could hardly hope to recruit Indians for the missions or to keep them in the missions. That is why the Spanish plans provided for sending small numbers of soldiers and settlers along with the Franciscan missionaries.

Within the over-all scheme of missions, there were a number of variations possible that gave rise to a series of questions. Some arose over the precise role and location of the military garrisons. Should the presidios be placed within the boundaries of the missions, or at some distance from them, or should the garrisons be divided? What should be the relation between the friars and the soldiers—that is, who commanded whom? In what circumstances could one call for help from the other? The question was more complicated than one might think, for if the missionaries sometimes needed military help, the military needed supplies of food and detachments of workers from the missions. A further military desire, which the Franciscans could not regard as a need, was access to Indian women. Other questions arose over the matter of Hispanic settlers. Should there be more than the barest minimum needed to provide population for a few Spanish towns? In Paraguay, for example, the Jesuits, with royal approval, tried to keep out all Spanish settlers. When they were found intruding into the mission area, they were arrested and expelled. If more than the bare minimum of Hispanic settlement was permitted, the settlers would take over Indian lands and try to seize the Indian men for labor and the Indian women for concubinage. Behind all these questions lay perhaps the most fundamentally serious: To what extent was Indian life to be changed? In the areas of high culture in Mexico, the changes brought by Spanish conquest and Christianization could be relatively limited. Aboriginal religious beliefs had to be rooted out, but native economy, much of native social structure, and even native government could be retained.

In California, with its multitude of Indian groups, speaking many languages, with little social stratification, a limited political organization, and a primitive, non-agricultural technology, the changes had to be sweeping. The Indians would have to be grouped into new communities, taught agriculture, stockraising, and new crafts as well as a new religion, and thus would have to be kept under a firm control that would leave little unsupervised. The other decisions in Spanish planning were that Spanish settlement would be restricted to a small number of people grouped in a very few towns, that the Spanish military garrisons or presidios would be placed near enough to the missions to rush to their aid if needed but far away enough so that the Indians and soldiers would be kept separate. The exact nature of command between military and missionaries was never settled satisfactorily, and actual working relations varied from cordial cooperation through reluctant assistance rendered with frigid dislike, to what the missionaries regarded as sabotage.

Missionary work in California began in 1769. A chain of missions in Lower California, originally Jesuit but by then in the hands of Franciscans, was turned over to Dominicans to free the Franciscans for work farther north. The Dominicans agreed to provide from Lower California supplies and livestock for the new missions. Additional Franciscan missionaries came from a special training college in Mexico City, the College of San Fernando. Father Junípero Serra set out with a mixed expedition of friars, soldiers, settlers, and livestock from the northernmost mission in Lower California. The expedition reached the site of San Diego and founded the first mission of San Diego de Alcalá on July 16, 1769. In 1969 we celebrated the bicentenary.

There is no need here to go into the story of the missions, which has been written often and at great length. We should notice that the chain of missions came into being rather slowly. When Father Serra died in 1784, there were in existence nine missions. Of those he founded five. During the course of the following decades, new missions were established in spurts: there would be a period of years without the founding of a mission, and then from one to three would be built. The last of the missions, founded on July 4, 1823, was San Francisco Solano at Sonoma. The Spanish plan had been that the missions be founded approximately one day's journey apart. In the end the chain came close to achieving that plan, but, during the period of Spanish royal rule, there were long marches of several days' duration between missions. The missions were concentrated along the coast, and in general brought under Spanish control the Indians of the coast.

In the missions the Indians were brought to a completely new life. There were certain differences between central and northern California, on the one hand, and California south of San Fernando Mission in the San Fernando Valley, on the other. In the north the Indians were settled around the mission buildings. In the south they were brought together into little settlements called *ranchorillas* at some distance from the mission complex; they tended to remain on their old lands and lived in these villages with slightly more freedom. But however the Indians were settled, north and south, they were completely under the control of the Franciscan friars, who ordered their lives with a firm hand. The Indians were put into new housing planned by the missionaries, and their work and recreation were directed by the friars. Married couples had separate quarters, but if they lived at the mission itself, they frequently received their food from a communal kitchen. Girls above the age of puberty were put into what was called the *monjerillo,* the monastic establishment, a large room in which they were locked at night. They worked under supervision and were always carefully watched by older women. The unmarried men lived in other quarters in the mission compound and could move in and out more freely, but if any attempted to leave the mission without permission, they were hunted down and brought back.

All Indian life was organized in new communal patterns. The Indians were taught many new crafts, completely unknown to them before, by artisans brought from Mexico. Among the new crafts, for example, were tile-making, brick-making, carpentry with iron tools, furniture-making, house construction, the building of dams and irrigation works, the complex activities of raising crops with plows and draft animals, the raising of fruits and vegetables, and stockraising. A small number of Hispanic artisans and friars taught thousands of Indians a totally new way of life. The plan was that the Indians should raise their own food and supply themselves with all necessary items except for a few things that could not be produced locally. They were also to maintain the missionaries and furnish much of the food needed in the presidios. Such a drastic change in the Indians' way of life could only be brought about through steady supervision and steady direction, the friars working with the Indians and watching over them. The missionaries had help, of course, from hired artisans and particularly from the soldiers detailed directly to the mission—normally six men to a mission. One of the soldiers was usually given the title of master of works (in effect, chief foreman), and he became particularly responsible for teaching the Indians and supervising their work.

The Franciscan missionaries were carrying out a theory of Christianization which has been elaborated in our time at the University of Louvain. To be made truly Christian, the Indians had to be brought into a situation in which at every point in life, whether they looked for food, wanted arts, worked at crafts, or whether they went to church, to a ceremony, to an amusement or diversion—whatever it might be—they were surrounded and pervaded by the new religion. The old heathen customs and ways must be suppressed relentlessly, but there must never be a vacuum that might be filled either by error or by a later return to heathen beliefs. In the first years, the Franciscans even tried to suppress Indian assemblies and dances. After a while, however, they realized that the Indians had to be left some outlet for releasing emotion, and so later the missionaries even encouraged dances, but always supervised them. In the later years, the missionaries also permitted the Indians short periods of retirement to the bush, but made sure that they returned.

The missions in the last resource obviously relied upon coercion. Many of the Indians were locked into rooms at night. Those Indians who did not obey or who broke discipline were flogged, put in stocks, jailed, or punished in other ways. If the missionaries could not handle the trouble, the military were called in. If the Indians ran away, they were hunted down and brought back.

There was inevitably some Indian reaction. Numbers of Indians tried to flee. There were even riots and a few, a very few, actual revolts. The worst of the revolts occurred in the earliest years at San Diego, but there were others. The missionaries varied greatly in personality: some were tactful and thoughtful; others were abrupt and harsh. Much of the Indians' reaction depended upon the personalities of the missionaries in their particular mission, in accordance with a principle true in almost all human relations. The kind of reaction varied between those Indians who had been brought in from a heathen life and those who were born at the mission. Those who knew another life could think of running away; those born at the mission had far less sense of the possibility of another kind of life, and tended more merely to play hookey, although some did try to flee to the Indians of the interior.

The longer-term effects of the missions were clearly that the Indians were Christianized, and with each generation the new religion sank in more deeply. The Indians were Hispanized to a very great extent even though most of them did not learn Spanish. There was interbreeding with whites, partly through the garrisons, since the soldiers sought out Indian women despite the objections of the friars. Another and very important effect, which the Spanish did not plan, was that they brought the whole array of Old World diseases to a population which had no previous exposure or acquired resistance. The result was cataclysmic. The missions probably would have been depopulated within one or two generations if the Spanish military had not gone inland to the coastal ranges and even to the interior valleys for more Indians. The missions were able to keep up the numbers of their Indians only by steady, forced recruiting. Another element that must be mentioned, although we cannot easily assess its action, was psychic upset, for the Indians were moved very rapidly from one way of life to another, under rigid control, with very little voice in what went on. There is much evidence to show the presence of such upset, if only in the number of fugitives and the extent to which the Spanish had to resort to punishment.

From what has been said, it is clear that there are various ways of looking at the missions. One is the idea of a Spanish Arcadia, where the friars preached and the Indians docilely went about their work. There is probably some truth in this idea. Another conception looks to the coercion and violent change. It also has truth in it. But one very important aspect must be noticed, and that is that the mission system provided a substantial place for the Indians in society. Although they were at the bottom of the social pyramid and their life was completely remade, they were a necessary part of society. The missions existed for them, and the friars, even though their powers were ample, were trustees for their charges.

Let us turn now to the Spanish civil population and the Indians, for these relations were different from those in the missions. I include the military in the Spanish civil population. Among the people who came from Mexico, there were a few upper-class persons—the officers—but not many. Most of the soldiers were various mixtures of European, Indian, and Negro. In Mexico, they would have been in the lower social strata. But in California they were in a new area where they could hope to rise in the social scale, for there were other people who could be pushed into the lowest places in society. The Spanish civil population regarded the Indians as labor and as a source of women. That was not the role planned for the Indians by the missionaries. It was not that the missionaries objected to intermarriage, quite the contrary, but the Spanish civil population by and large did not want marriage; it wanted temporary relations that could be broken at will, or even the equivalent of harems. Despite the opposition of the missionaries, many of the Spanish men had their way. The friars could not always control the soldiers, and furthermore Indians from the missions had to be furnished the soldiers

and settlers for work. The missionaries did demand that the
Indians be returned when they had completed a tour of duty. In
a few years, however, the Spanish civil population began to establish ranches and larger towns, for which they wanted Indians as
laborers, settled on the premises and outside mission control.

The Spanish civil population, then, had somewhat different
ideas from those of the missionaries, but they still saw the Indians
as an integral part of society, a lower class that would support
them and minister to them. I should point out that their conception of the Indians' role in society was simply that of the role
of the lower class in contemporary Mexico and Europe. The
Indians were not being discriminated against as Indians; they
were simply being given the same treatment that lower classes
elsewhere received.

The end of Spanish rule and the establishment of an independent Mexican government in 1821 brought some changes. The
civil population, which was steadily increasing in size, had a much
freer hand in dealing with the Indians, whereas the missionaries
no longer were able to count upon backing from the new government. In the 1830's, the Mexican Republic decided to liquidate
the missions. The missionaries were to become parish priests
restricted to ordinary religious ministrations. The Indian lands
were to be turned over to civilian administrators who were to be
guardians for the Indians. As far as possible, the Indian settlements were to become formal towns, with their own governments. The mission lands were to become the lands of the new
towns, either to be assigned to individual Indians or to be farmed
in common, with a reserve held back for use as pasture and for
further assignment. That was the plan. What happened was that,
although the missions were indeed ended as a system, the new
administrators took everything. They seized the lands to such an
extent that lands were not even granted to other Mexicans; they
set up their own ranches, and they attempted to force the Indians
to work for them. Many of the Indians fled to the back country,
some melted into the general Hispanized population, and per-

haps two or three thousand out of the 20,000 then in the missions remained as workers for the administrators. They became the traditional peons of Mexican society. Again, it was not that they were exploited as Indians but rather as a lower class. Between 1832 and 1845, the conceptions of the Hispanic civil population became the dominant policy.

There remains to be discussed the larger part of California, the interior, which was not under Hispanic control. The whole Hispanic period from 1769 to 1821 was one in which the Hispanic people were pressing northward along the coast and slowly penetrating the coast range and the central valley. After nearly three-quarters of a century of such penetration, that is, by 1846, most of the present state of California was still not under the control of the Hispanic population. The Indians of the interior were, on the whole, peaceful and gentle people, as indeed all California Indians were. Very small numbers of Spanish were able to dominate relatively large numbers of Indians in the interior as on the coast. Spanish expeditions ranged the interior to find fugitives and to recruit Indians for the missions by force. Since the Spanish did not remain in the interior to control it, however, Indian reaction there was different. The Indians became acquainted with European ways more slowly. One example is the way they learned about livestock. At first they thought the animals simply another kind of game to be killed and eaten as, for instance, they ate the first horses. With time, as they learned that cattle were for eating and horses for riding, they began to acquire horses for riding and began to raid Hispanic settlements and ranches to pick up livestock. They also learned the meaning of firearms, but, since the Spanish had a very careful policy of never permitting the Indians to get hold of them and closely watched trade in arms, the Indians had far more trouble in obtaining such weapons. Nevertheless, by the 1840's there was building up in the interior of California a reinvigorated and changed Indian society that was developing the tactics and the means for coping with Hispanic settlers. Had there been no political change, a new Apache culture probably would have developed that would have given as good an account of itself as the Apaches and Commanches of the Southwest did in their defence against the Mexicans and Anglo-Americans. But this does not mean that the interior Indians did not suffer any harm from the Hispanic settlement of California. Communication with mission Indians who fled to the interior and the movements of Spanish expeditions certainly spread disease, which once among the interior Indians spread from group to group. Hispanic raids killed and seized people. So there was damage, balanced by adaptation.

In 1846 the annexation of California to the United States brought an end to the Hispanic period. At that time, in the part of California under Hispanic control, there were at maximum 6,000 *gente de razón,* people considered fully part of the Hispanic community and subject to the ordinary action of the laws. Perhaps 4,500 people were Hispanic, that is, people of European, Mexican, Indian, and Negro stock in a wide range of mixtures. Included in the mixtures were already some elements of California Indian. Perhaps 1,500 people were Anglo-Americans who had settled in California under the Mexican regime. The survivors of the mission Indians by then were down to a few thousand, perhaps 5,000 at a guess. The total number of the Indians in the present area of the state was perhaps 200,000, most of whom were in the interior. If the Indian population in 1769 had been 300,000, perhaps 100,000 had died out through the European presence.

We can see that the same process that had taken place in Mexico from the time of Cortés was taking place in California. The Indians were suffering massive losses in numbers, mostly through disease. At the same time, they were undergoing incorporation into Hispanic society as a class of laborers, peasants, and servants. They were slowly learning Spanish and interbreeding with Hispanic people. They were treated with the brutality that characterized the ordinary class relations of the eighteenth century in Europe and Latin America. But they were given a place in the new society and were regarded as one of its indispensable elements.

Selected Questions and Answers

Q. "Would you compare the population density of the California Indians to another part of America?"

A. "Indian population was obviously sparse in California—something on the order of one to two people per square mile. The population of other parts of America at the time of the coming of the Europeans is at this point wildly controversial. For some parts of the Caribbean, such as Hispaniola, estimates range as high as 300 per square mile. In Mexico, we calculate it at about 125 per square mile. Other areas would not have had more than one to every ten square miles, depending on food resources. The area of the United States is thought to have had from half a million to a million Indians, but there are people who say this figure is far too low. Compared to densities in Europe or Africa at the same time, the density in California or the United States would be very low."

Q. "Could you compare or contrast the Negro on the plantation with the Indian in the mission?"

A. "Let me say first that the Indian in the mission in California was different from the Indian in the mission in Paraguay or the Indian in the mission in northern Mexico. We really have to examine the Indian's situation region by region. The plantation also was very different. The policies pursued on the plantations, the policies for acquiring slaves, were different. Normally we think of the Anglo-American mainland as a chamber of horrors. It may have been. But by applying one simple and interesting test which is practically never used—Does the population find life so unbearable that it does not reproduce itself?—we get another view. For the Negroes on the plantations of the Anglo-American mainland reproduced and steadily increased in numbers, whereas elsewhere, particularly on the sugar plantations in the Caribbean, they tended to die out. Now the sugar plantation was a fairly industrialized form of activity, and sugar plantations tended to buy two to four times as many men as women, so we would have to compare the breeding females in the two groups and what happened to them. That, by the way, has not been done.

"The Anglo-American plantation built up a set of laws which attempted to regard the Negro as a domestic animal without personality. It was unable to do so in practice, however, and a series of conventional adjustments took place underneath the law. Spanish law did attempt to provide the Negro with a personality, although he was regarded as civilly dead. That was the rule of all European law. But in practice, the Spanish plantation owner circumvented the codes and restrictions that were provided by law. I have found little evidence to suggest that if we compared a Cuban sugar plantation around 1840, at the height of industrialized sugar raising, and a commercialized cotton plantation in Mississippi around 1840, we could make a case for either one as better than the other. Slavery always created a situation in which the owner tended to use his power to the maximum; but if he was shrewd, he looked to his domestic animals, and in the end, if he wanted labor, he came to a series of adjustments with his labor force. In many parts of the system, what really existed underneath the legal statements was a tribal encampment in a series of customary arrangements with the owner. If we look at the Caribbean today and at what has emerged from the ruins of the plantation system, we can see that a whole series of conventional arrangements existed under slavery, such as the Sunday market and the right to provision grounds. Most studies of slavery are carried out in an atmosphere of hysteria, and people are too busy proving points or writing propaganda to look at things objectively. Obviously, I am not making a plea for slavery, but I do think that we must study it in a careful, objective way that will not distort the evidence.

"Now, mission Indians in some parts of the world were held in slavery or in peonage. Once the civil administrators took over in California, there was no question that that happened here. But the treatment they received varied greatly, and the missionaries, whatever their faults, earnestly tried to work on behalf of the Indians. They tried; their ideas were not always the best."

Q. "What would you consider the most objective treatment of the Indians? The Department of Anthropology stresses the Indians' side, and it seems that History is always tending to emphasize the Spanish or colonial side."

A. "Let me start by saying that God, until recent times, has never been kind to the lower classes because it is always the upper classes who write the records. This creates an automatic and almost unbeatable bias in favor of the upper-class point of view. Next, I do not know what your standard of reference for 'objective treatment' is, for behind the question you ask is another which is not easily answered, and that is, 'What is a valid standard?' There we get to questions to theology, for only in theology at this time are we able to come to any statement about what a valid standard of reference is. All that one can do is to state the standard that he will use, and, in cases in which several are obviously of equal merit, point out the relation of each to the evidence. The Department of Anthropology is on perfectly good ground; the Department of History is also on perfectly good ground. We have no means of choosing at this point."

Q. "How did the Europeans and the Indians communicate? Did the Indians learn Spanish?"

A. "Enough Indians learned Spanish and enough Europeans learned Indian tongues for communication, but on the whole surprisingly few of the California Indians learned much Spanish. Many Indians had small Spanish vocabularies so that they could communicate in the most important things. Those who were taken into Mexican or Spanish families as servants obviously learned more, and their children probably knew even better Spanish, but this affected a very small proportion of the Indian population."

Q. "You mentioned resistance among the Indians brought to the missions in terms of flight and some riots or revolts. Were they ever organized to any extent?"

A. "The revolt at San Diego was certainly organized, and there was a revolt at Buenaventura which had elements of organization. Elsewhere such efforts at resistance as occurred were much smaller affairs. The flights sometimes involved fairly large groups, but generally there was not a wholesale exodus."

Q. "Was the organization among the Indians based on any organization that had existed among the groups before the missionaries took them over? Was there some kind of hierarchy that they developed among themselves?"

A. "The missionaries tended to put people of the same linguistic group together, although some missions had several linguistic groups. Obviously Indians of the same linguistic group could get together more easily, and the serious uprising at San Diego fundamentally involved one group."

Q. "When the Franciscans came and more or less Christianized the Indians, were there, as in Mexico, many Indian elements in the Christianization of the Indians?"

A. "You are asking about what we call 'syncretism.' We are still arguing about how much took place in Mexico. There are several views. One is 'idols behind the altars.' Another sees a beneficent and harmless adaptation in which insignificant elements of native observance were allowed to be retained.

"Obviously, in the length of time the missions were here, eradication of Indian beliefs must have been very difficult and there must have been considerably greater survival of the old beliefs in California than in Mexico. The exact extent of it, I cannot really say. The religion of the Indians, as it has survived, is Catholicism with certain festivals which retain marked Indian characteristics. But the continuing operations of parish priests have also continued to implant Christianity and to eradicate the most obnoxiously heathen elements. Christianization did not stop in 1846."

Q. "If the Indian was regarded as lower class, what were his chances of moving up?"

A. "Absolutely nil. It would have taken several generations and would have meant first the adoption of Hispanic ways. Here we get into the value system of Roman society and the later societies based upon Roman tradition. One qualifies for social advancement by adopting the ways of the upper class. This is shown in speech, in dress, in the possession of a suitable fortune, and in the possession of a suitable education. Whatever barriers lie in the possession of a darker skin can be overcome by a university degree, a fortune, or a high enough government post so that one's favor is worth cultivating. The Roman pattern obtains today in Mexico, but there simply was not the time for it to operate in California."

Q. "I cannot understand why the Indians entered the missions. Obviously they were in the majority. Weren't the missionaries at a disadvantage?"

A. "The missionaries came into a very peaceful society with very little power of resistance and no organization for resistance. There was also the attraction of the new, added to coercion."

Q. "In our elementary classes, we use state texts and we teach about the missions, and we paint a very lovely picture. As I sit here and listen to you, I find it all so wrong."

A. "No, it is half wrong, half right."

Q. "What should we teach?"

Q. "Excuse me, please. I also teach fourth grade and I probably use the same textbook that the others do. I think that in this particular area as in any other area you teach, you must teach the book and then add what the book leaves out."

A. "Well, I think here you have to give both sides of the mission. There was much about it that was idyllic; the intentions were certainly honorable. There is simply no use in blaming people for not knowing the germ theory before anyone in the world knew about germs. The eighteenth century was just another society, with other views and other conceptions."

Q. "Was capital punishment used against the California Indians around the missions or presidios?"

A. "Yes, in a very few cases. Professor Cook has tabulated all known instances of punishment, and there were a few cases of capital punishment."

Q. "There were Anglo-American travelers in California who mentioned a vaquero class that seems to have been somewhere between the *gente de razón* and the Indians—that is, the cowboys or workers on the ranches who seem to have had a certain amount of mobility. Where did they come from? Did they really exist?"

A. "There were vaqueros, and my own impression is that they were counted to a great extent among the *gente de razón*. But Indians were also used as vaqueros, and they remained Indians."

Chapter II

The California Indian and Anglo-American Culture

Sherburne F. Cook

"It was one of the last human hunts in history, and the basest and most brutal of them all." Thus did Hubert Howe Bancroft, patriarch of California historians, describe relations between the citizens of the United States of America and the California Indians. The Gold Rush and subsequent economic activity brought American white men into the interior of California, which had been largely neglected by the Spanish and Mexicans. American rule, therefore, greatly expanded the disasterous effects of European diseases upon the Indians and the disruption of their native hunting and gathering territories. The Anglo-Americans brought to California a heritage of fear and hatred of Indians bred by the long conflict on the American frontier. Unlike Spanish America, the United States did not depend on Indians as a prime source of labor, and the social and political system of the United States never established a well-defined status for the red man.

It is not surprising, then, that in this chapter on Indian-American relations, Dr. Sherburne F. Cook describes an attitude of "implacable hatred of the red race." Dr. Cook is Emeritus Professor of Physiology at the University of California, Berkeley. Among his many published works are *Conflict Between the California Indian and White Civilization* and (with W. W. Borah) *The Aboriginal Population of Central Mexico on the Eve of the Spanish Conquest.*

The California Indian and Anglo-American Culture

On September 15, 1855, the Commanding General of the United States forces in California, J. E. Wool, wrote to Indian Agent T. J. Henley concerning conditions at Fort Jones on the Klamath River.[1] At that point were gathered " . . . some hundred and fifty men, women and children, whose husbands have been killed by the white inhabitants of California . . . ." The General then went on, " . . . It appears to me that something ought to be done for these miserable creatures, who it appears were not in the wrong, and whom the white inhabitants are determined to exterminate."

This was the same Agent Henley who wrote to the Office of Indian Affairs on December 4, 1858, in support of the forcible removal of two hundred Tulare Lake Indians by local ranchers to the Fresno Reservation, for, as he put it, "abide with us they shall not."[2] Not long afterward, on April 29, 1864, the San Francisco *Bulletin* quoted the Mendocino (Ukiah) *Herald* of April 22 as advocating the complete removal of all Indians to some very remote spot "or to an island in the sea." Any escaping this fate should be slaughtered outright, said the *Herald*.

These are fair samples of public opinion in the 1850's and 1860's for the solution of the most pressing contemporary race problem: what to do with the native inhabitants of the Golden State. The type of thinking they manifest is so contrary to most modern ideas concerning race relations that it becomes necessary to examine the background and culture of the people who made up the dominant population.

In the years following California's occupation by the United States, the social environment of the region underwent a rapid transition from Hispanic culture, as expressed primarily in the mission system, to the culture of the Anglo-Americans, who had been entering in great numbers even prior to the Gold Rush. Another article in this series, by Professor Woodrow W. Borah, has set forth the characteristics of the Ibero-American religio-political organization and its operation with respect to the aboriginal occupants of the territory. He has pointed out that the essential policy was one of conservation and utilization of the native. Despite the occasional appeal to violence, and a certain inherent ruthlessness, the Hispanic Californian attempted to gain two objectives: first, to convert the native race to Christianity, and, second, to exploit it as a great labor pool underlying the superstructure of white society. In theory at least, the Indian was, or should have become, a citizen, although perhaps of second class. In the long run, even this distinction would have vanished, for the Mexicans of Spanish origin felt no social or personal aversion to free intermarriage with the Indian. Even when confronting the unreduced, relatively wild tribes of the interior, both civilian and military groups, despite a sometimes liberal use of force, undertook to bring the native within the framework of a Europeanized society, rather than destroy him forthwith.

A profound change occurred when the Anglo-Americans submerged the Hispanic population, replaced its form of government, and drove its culture into the remnants of the missions and ranchos. The "Norteamericanos," as the Mexicans call them, had been engaged for two hundred years in murderous warfare with the indigenous peoples of North America. First came the struggle for a foothold, and then the long, slow, crushing advance over the breadth of a continent. The initial armed hostility rapidly crystallized a fundamental intolerance into an implacable hatred of the red race. This hatred was inflamed by the very competent resistance offered by the tribes of the Mississippi and Missouri basins, a resistance thoroughly punctuated by excessive atrocity on both sides.

When the pioneers who had crossed the plains reached the Pacific Coast, their unalterable policy toward the natives, any natives, had come to embody a point of view diametrically opposed to that of the Hispanic occupants of the area. While the latter had paid much attention to the religious welfare of the Indian, the Anglo-Americans were completely indifferent. While the Indian had supplied the basic labor for the Ibero-American economic system, in that of North America he was given no place, or at best was relegated to abject serfdom. While the Spaniard or Mexican found no moral or physical obstacle to marriage with the native, the American pioneer abjured such unions with finality, and regarded those who entered into them as beyond the pale of social recognition. Together with this repulsion, there developed the doctrine, accepted by many people, that the Indian was inherently, congenitally wicked, a soul inevitably lost to damnation. Such a belief must have been that of D. N. Cooley, Indian Agent at the Tule River Farm, when he wrote in his annual report: "A cruel, cowardly vagabond, given to thieving, gambling, drunkenness, and all that is vicious, without one redeeming trait, is a true picture of the California Digger . . . ."[3]

It is difficult for us now to grasp the depth of the feeling which motivated the first North American settlers of California, an animosity which reached almost the level of a mass psychosis. Nevertheless, it is worthwhile to make the attempt, because this feeling still persists in attentuated form to the present day, and in the meantime it has colored the relations between the white man and not only the red man but almost all other ethnic stocks as well.

It was highly unfortunate that the hostility of the Anglo-Americans in California should have been directed against an aboriginal population which was fundamentally peaceful and relatively inoffensive. The work of Alfred L. Kroeber and his colleagues has demonstrated that internal fighting among the Pacific Coast tribes was trivial and of rare occurrence. This conclusion is reinforced by the fact that Portola and Serra, in 1769, with scarcely more than one hundred men, were able to penetrate to the Golden Gate, found several missions, and occupy an area inhabited by 50,000 to 100,000 natives, all with no single incident involving the use of weapons. The followers of these explorers, supported only by a few score priests and soldiers, were able to consolidate the coastal strip from San Diego to San Francisco and bring the entire Indian population into the mission system with no more than two or three relatively minor physical conflicts. Indeed, it was not until fifty years after the first expeditions, when the heathen tribes of the central valleys obtained the horse and gun, that any serious attacks were made upon the Spanish and Mexican settlements. Moreover, we may note that there is on record no case in which the natives offered armed resistance upon the *first entry* of the whites into any region. It was not until close contact had developed friction between the races that anything approaching open warfare occurred.

During the period of Mexican control, from 1820 to 1845, immigration of both Ibero- and Anglo-Americans increased sharply, although by 1845 there were still no more than a few thousand white people in the entire state. During this period it is also true that relations between the races deteriorated substantially. The factors responsible for this negative trend included the destruction of the missions, with dispersal of the neophytes, and an increasing penetration of the interior river valleys by cattlemen and fur traders. This process was accentuated by the formation of huge landed estates such as those of Sutter, Yount, Bidwell, and Savage. Nevertheless, it is probable that some sort of *modus vivendi* would have been worked out, had not two other forces suddenly been brought into operation.

The first was the wave of immigration from the eastern states, a movement which actually had preceded the annexation of California, had attained considerable strength by 1848, and was accelerating with great rapidity. The second was the inrush of gold seekers, which began in 1849 and brought fully 100,000 persons into the region within a year or two. The net result was a mushroom growth to a figure of close to a quarter of a million by 1851, a mass of people who overrode not only the Indians but also the native white population of California.

Some idea of what happened to the Indians may be obtained merely by following their numbers through the nineteenth century. A reasonable estimate would put approximately 250,000 aboriginal inhabitants in the state just prior to 1769. During the Spanish and Mexican era, there was severe attrition among those living along the central coast, on the rivers of the open San Joaquin Valley, and in southern California. Most of the casualties were referable to the disruption of native society locally, and to the generally high mortality inflicted by introduced diseases. By the end of the war with Mexico, the Indian population of the coastal region south of San Francisco probably had been reduced to no more than 40,000 with perhaps another 10,000 clinging to their homes on Tulare and Buenavista Lakes, as well as along the lower courses and delta of the San Joaquin and Sacramento Rivers.

The remainder, who amounted to some 125,000, still existed relatively undisturbed in the northern coast ranges, up the Klamath River, across the mountains to Shasta, and down the Sierra Nevada foothills all the way to the Tehachapi. It was precisely these regions that were inundated by the Gold Rush, for the miners penetrated to every stream from which an ounce of gold could be panned.

The depletion of the natives was catastrophic. Firm estimates of the population in detail are not available until 1880, at which time conditions had stabilized sufficiently to permit a fairly good count. By this date there cannot have been over 20,000 Indians left, no more than two-thirds of whom lived in the mining areas. Thus, in 1873 the report of the Commissioner of Indian Affairs[4] estimated a total of 17,000, and, for 1880, C. Hart Merriam[5] put the figure at 16,500 for the state as a whole.

In the period since 1880, there has been a reversal and a tendency toward an increase. The comprehensive census of 1928 showed something like 25,000 persons who stated that they were of California Indian descent. For the distribution of the recent federal award resulting from the Claims case, it is anticipated that there will be from 30,000 to 40,000 applicants. This augmentation in number, however, has occurred primarily by virtue of an admixture with other races, which has produced a profound dilution of the aboriginal strain. For example, censuses taken at the Hupa Reservation Agency and the Mission Agency in 1940 showed respectively only 29 and 47 per cent of the people to be full-blooded Indians. On the other hand, approximately five per cent reported themselves to be only one-sixteenth or one-thirty-second Indian.

If we now examine more carefully the destruction of the Indian race in the mid-nineteenth century, we find that, apart from a probable fall in birth rate concerning which we have little factual knowledge, the chief causes appear to have been disease and rough treatment by the Americans.

The health factor had always been significant. Even prior to 1840, devastating epidemics of smallpox and malaria swept through the central valley and the coast ranges. Several thousand persons are reported to have died. Moreover, even at the missions, where living conditions were generally quite good, an extremely high mortality was caused by infections such as typhoid, measles, and tuberculosis, together with a virulent form of syphilis. These maladies, naturally, could not be confined to the mission environment, but quickly spread to the non-missionized tribes where they became endemic. The intensity of their attack upon the natives was amplified manyfold when the massive immigration of 1849 broadcast a host of new pathogens, with an accompaniment of universal bad sanitation, water pollution, and complete lack of social control. The ravages of disease, nevertheless, could probably have been tolerated without permanent and fatal consequences had the Indian not been subjected to a bitter interracial conflict with the Anglo-American, during the course of which he barely escaped extinction.

The actual destruction of life was most clearly manifested in military action. Small expeditions had been sent out for half a century by the Spanish and Mexican administrations to chastise and subdue recalcitrant natives in the interior. With the occupation of California by the United States Army in 1845–1848, however, such operations were greatly expanded, even though they still followed conventional lines. Bodies of troops at company strength were scattered through all parts of the territory, where they established "forts," the primary purpose of which was to hold in check and "pacify" the Indians. The latter, according to all previous experience on the continent, would soon initiate violent physical opposition. As one might expect, the least sign of armed hostility was countered by a crushing military campaign, in the course of which it was standard practice to burn the native villages and destroy all stored food.

During the 1850's, the army came to participate less and less in these affairs. The regular units were then replaced by local bodies of militia, acting under orders from the state, and eventually by groups of private citizens who went forth to fight the Indians clothed with little more authority than their own charitable inclinations. It would be of little value to recount in detail the series of atrocities perpetrated by these people, although there might be mentioned the notorious Clear Lake massacre in 1850 and the Humboldt Bay massacre in 1860. The former was committed by an army contingent under Captain (later General) Nathaniel Lyon, the latter by a company of local civilians. In both instances, several dozen helpless women and children were cut down without mercy.

The actual number of deaths directly referable to these operations is difficult to assess, but the available evidence leads to the conclusion that from 1848 to 1865 the casualties amounted to several (perhaps three to five) thousand Indians. At the same time there went on an insidious erosion due to personal homicide, the result of that ordinary, everyday quarrelling, fighting, and shooting, with or without benefit of liquor, which characterized the culture of the 1850's in California. The Indians were predestined victims, particularly since no white man was ever punished for killing one. The number of recorded cases reaches a few hundred, possibly not a huge total, but still suggestive of a precarious and brutal existence. In this context, it is illuminating to quote an item published in the *Alta California* (San Francisco) for August 8, 1854: "Two Indians were found murdered in our streets the past week, by persons unknown, and dumped into the common receptacle made and provided for such cases."

The effect of physical contact was not always sudden and violent death. More debilitating because more subtle was the steady movement of white settlers, farmers, cattlemen, and lumbermen, as well as miners, onto the lands held by the local Indian villages. First came displacement and dispossession with unceremonious explusion; then followed exclusion from the former home domains by means of barbed wire, dogs, and guns. The uprooting of ancient social units, with its unavoidable destitution, was a severe blow in numerous instances, but even more critical was the elimination of the primitive means of subsistence, together with the complete lack of any substitute.

The native sources of food were copious, but they required a precise adaptive mechanism on the part of the natives in order to be usable. The ecological balance over large areas was entirely destroyed by the newly-entering civilization. Big game was driven out or killed; the salmon runs were reduced by placer mining in the streams; the acorn reserves of the valleys and foothills were dissipated by farming operations. But the most serious damage was inflicted by the simple occupation of the land, which in turn meant the denial of its use to the former occupants. Over the long run, this progressive mass eviction generated a horde of displaced persons, who roved about the countryside or moved into the settlements, trying to exist by scavenging and beggary, living in hopeless squalor and poverty, driven all too often to robbery for survival itself.

The most repulsive physical affront offered to the natives was the widespread practice of kidnapping. Before the American occupation of California, the Spanish-speaking ranchers had periodically abducted adults from the still-heathen villages in order to augment their labor supply. But the English-speaking settlers developed the technique of kidnapping small children, who were then sold as servants to respectable families for prices ranging from thirty to two hundred dollars. By 1860, this trade had reached the dimensions of an industry. In an editorial on July 19, 1862, the Sacramento *Union* charged that the purveyors to this traffic were actually killing the parents to secure the children for sale, and that such a child might be seen in the house of every fourth white man. No exact figure can be determined, but a fair estimate puts the number of persons thus stolen at fully three thousand.

We may wonder today why this nefarious business was tolerated, for tolerated it was. Although several attempts were made to prosecute well-known offenders, legal technicalities and outright acquittals prevented any of them from being brought to punishment. Moreover, a large segment of public opinion held that the Indian children were much better off as virtual slaves in the well-to-do and good Christian atmosphere of the white families than they would have been suffering misery and starvation with their own parents.

Mention of the kidnapping problem leads to consideration of the entire social status accorded the red man in California by the dominant race. At the outset of such a discussion, it may be affirmed unequivocally that the physical violence and economic restriction visited upon the native was accompanied by a moral degradation such as has seldom been the lot of any minority group in the New World, not even of the Negro.

Civil liberty, as we understand the term, and as, even in 1850, it was embodied in the Constitution, literally did not apply to the Indian. He could not vote, he could not hold office, he could not attend a white school, he had no police protection, he was not permitted to testify in court, he could not accuse a white man of any legal infraction nor could he claim any damages for injury. As W. W. Robinson has eloquently described in his little book, *The Indians of Los Angeles*,[6] an Indian could be picked up without a warrant and could be held in jail without bail and upon no charge, except the ubiquitous offense of vagrancy. After his arrest, he might be put at labor on public works, or he might be put up at auction and his services as a laborer sold to the highest bidder for a period not to exceed four months, without compensation, except perhaps food. Another device was to invoke the so-called "indenture law," whereby any Indian adult, or child with the consent of his parents, could be legally bound over to a citizen for a long term of years. During this interval, his labor was enjoyed by the master in return for subsistence. If, at any time, the Indian absconded, he could be brought back by force and was liable for further punishment.

A particularly offensive but broadly illustrative case[7] of such peonage occured in Ukiah in 1865. A man in that town had hired an Indian to do a job. One day the Indian met a man named Bob Hildreth, who claimed him as his property. When the Indian said he was working for another man, Hildreth tied him to his horse and dragged him to death. Now Hildreth's claim was based upon the fact that he had bought the estate of the late Indian fighter, Captain Jarboe, from the widow. She stated that she had set Jarboe's Indians free after his death. But Hildreth maintained that they were part of the estate, and hence inalienable *under the apprentice law.*

One annoying problem concerned the use of intoxicating beverages. It is quite true that the Indian, under the influence of alcohol, was prone to display a release of inhibitions which, in turn, permitted him to commit acts of violence. Such behavior, to be sure, was not unknown among members of other races, but as demonstrated by the Indian it generated a strong reaction, possibly grounded in fear, on the part of white society. A serious attempt was made to prevent his access to alcohol, an attempt which was then, and has been ever since, only partially successful. Prohibition did not solve the problem, although it may have mitigated some of the worst effects, and the liquor laws are still a source of irritation alike to local authorities and to Indians.

A much more profound manifestation of oppression was in the area of sex. For several years following 1849, California was subjected to a tremendous influx of unattached males, seeking gold, a high proportion of whom were of the worst personal character. As always happens under such circumstances, these men resorted without restraint to native women, and used force, even homicide, when any resistance was offered. Most of these affairs were wholly casual. On the other hand, many whites took Indian women as concubines and lived with them in domesticity for extended periods, thereby earning for themselves as a class the name of "squaw men." There are reported to have been hundreds, if not thousands, of such cases.

However, before we condemn too severely this very common form of extra-marital relationship, we should recognize certain facts. First, we can not deny the almost complete lack of suitable white women during the first years after the Gold Rush. Second, we must not overlook the extremely rigid sexual morality which characterized the middle and upper levels of Anglo-American society during the Victorian era. Third, we must remember that matrimony as a legal institution was unknown to the aboriginal Californian. Primitive marriage involved various types of ceremony, but ethnographic study and contemporary testimony both agree that wedlock in the Christian sense had no meaning whatever to the unconverted inhabitants. Hence the cohabitation of the "squaw man" and the Indian woman, provided that it was voluntarily undertaken, was entirely in accordance with "Indian custom," and was in no way offensive to native decorum. Nevertheless, if force was employed or pre-existing native families were disrupted, the moral and psychic trauma was serious.

After the mid-century, as California began to attract more and more sober, responsible immigrants from the eastern United States, people who came to establish homes, not to mine gold, the atrocities which were being inflicted upon the Indians and the ruthless exploitation to which they were being subjected began to evoke a significant counter-reaction. On a small scale, there were sporadic and largely abortive attempts to bring local relief, encouraged by a good deal of preaching from the pulpits and editorializing by the newspapers of the cities. Groups of interested citizens here and there made collections of food and clothing for the benefit of the most destitute and conspicuous of the victims. Some of the important ranchers took pride in maintaining good living standards for their colonies of Indian labor.

In the meantime, there had grown up in the older, northern states a fairly strong humanitarian movement, directed primarily toward the abolition of Negro slavery, but also advocating civilized treatment of Indians. However, it had become very clear on the Pacific Coast that unorganized private charity, even coupled with quite a powerful body of public opinion, could not cope effectively with the distress of many thousand potential and actual indigents. For a time, and predominantly in the rural areas, the idea of literal, physical extermination of the red race was seriously entertained, an idea which was intensified by the long legacy of contempt and hatred which had been drilled into the heads of most Anglo-American immigrants. Fortunately, however, this solution, at least on a legalized basis and as official policy, was rejected. For a substitute, the white population was forced to turn to the only political entity which could or would introduce and maintain a substantial measure of assistance, the government of the United States.

The efforts of the various federal agencies to alleviate the lot of the California Indians present a tale of well-meaning incompetence, stolid indifference, and cynical maliciousness of which no American can be particularly proud.

The official entrance of national authority was made by the army as a military measure which accompanied the war with Mexico. The primary purpose was to secure the territory politically. A secondary function was to subjugate the native peoples and hold them harmless to the immigrants from the United States, as we previously outlined. The formal conquest was sealed by the treaty of Guadalupe Hidalgo, in 1848, one provision of which, amazingly enough, recognized the claim of the California Indians to recompense for lost lands. This concession was reinforced by acts of Congress in 1850 and 1851 which appropriated fifty thousand dollars to pay for negotiations with these Indians.

It will be remembered that the standard, but rather naive, procedure at that time was first to subdue the natives by armed force, and then, in European fashion, to bind the victory with a written treaty. The fact that untutored aborigines had no concept of the significance of a treaty, and understood only the capacity for the exercise of brute power, was immaterial to federal officials, military and civilian alike. In California the customary routine was followed. Three commissioners, Barbour, McKee, and Wozencraft, traversed the state in 1851 and secured eighteen treaties signed by representatives of the larger tribes. Among the provisions of each was compensation in the form of lands to be allocated to the dispossessed groups.

When, in 1852, President Fillmore recommended the eighteen treaties for ratification by the United States Senate, the California legislature objected violently, claiming that the lands in question were worth one hundred million dollars. This objection, plus some very strong pressure exerted by the California senators, resulted in the rejection of the treaties. Furthermore, in the name of "security," they were classified as secret and remained unavailable for public inspection until the year 1905.

When the door was thus abruptly closed upon any legal or honorable recompense for the injuries received by the natives, there remained only the reservation system, newly established under the Office of Indian Affairs.

It is popularly supposed that the reservations of the nineteenth century were little more than concentration camps. It must be admitted that at their worst, and far too often, they showed a close degree of resemblance. On the other hand, the theory upon which they were based was relatively enlightened and represented the best that humanitarian sentiment could expect in an era when shooting, burning, hanging, and scalping were commonplace events. Behind their inception lay an official, legalistic doctrine not unlike what we see today in regional districts, urban redevelopment, freeways, and other devices for improvement and "progress." The argument ran with the Indians, as it does now with the owners of condemned property, that, in the interest of the public welfare, they had been forcibly deprived of homes, food, and means of subsistence. In all equity these things should be replaced by something just as good.

The great vacant areas west of the Mississippi River seemed to provide sufficient raw land for full resettlement. The fact was recognized that the new occupants would have to be given help if they were to become established and support themselves under the American economic and agricultural system. Hence they were to be supplied with tools, with seed, and with building materials. The agents and other staff were charged with the responsibility for maintaining proper standards of public health and law enforcement as well as for instructing the tenants in the intricacies of American rural life. On paper, the system probably was as good as could have been devised under the existing conditions. Nevertheless, as applied to California, and as there administered, it was a complete failure for a generation and was notable for extraordinary abuses.

Perhaps the most critical reason for the collapse of the earlier reservations was the peculiar political organization of the California Indians, and the total disregard by white officialdom of their ancient habitats, material culture, and native languages. As was ably expounded by Professor Kroeber in the Claims case, California was unique in the United States with respect to the structure of its indigenous society. While, to the east, one found substantial tribes or confederacies such as the Iroquois, Sioux, or Apache, along the Pacific Coast were scattered dozens of little units, often no more than single villages, to which Kroeber applied the name "tribelets." There was no superior controlling class, such as ruled the Aztec or the Inca, nor any significant intergroup coordination. Each unit was confined to its own clearly recognized home, with an adjacent territory for foraging of not more than a few miles in extent. To tear out such a tribelet, *in toto,* and transport it to a far place and strange surroundings, inflicted a profound emotional injury. Moreover, it was customary for the army and the Indian Service to gather together the scraps and remnants of a dozen different linguistic stocks and throw them together in a confused mass at an undeveloped, unprepared reservation. Even today, at Round Valley, may be found descendants of local Yuki, Pomo from Sonoma County, Athabascans from Humboldt County, and Wintun or Maidu from the Sacramento Valley, all of whom once spoke quite different languages.

This unthinking displacement and reshuffling was carried out in the most harsh and callous manner. The victims were conducted under guard and were permitted to exist for days without adequate clothing, food, or shelter, both en route and after arrival at their destinations. Editorials frequently appeared in the San Francisco newspapers deploring the destitution of the Indians who were being brought from interior points through the city for delivery at reservations in the northern coast counties.

It is not surprising that those taken to reservations attempted to escape as soon as it was physically possible. Many contemporary press accounts and official reports attest to the fact that hundreds were escaping and returning as best they might to their ancient homes. Many of them were recaptured, sometimes repeatedly, and taken back to the reservations. Indeed, the extent of fugitivism reached such a level that some of the new resettlement areas had to be closed down permanently for sheer lack of occupants.

Once established upon the reservations, the Indians found it very difficult to develop any settled economy or social organization because of incessant attacks and harassment by the neighboring white population. These people bitterly resented the removal of good land for the use of the despised Indians. Repeated instances are on record of outright invasion and appropriation of sizeable tracts for farming, as well as of unrestrained trespass for the ranging of livestock. These measures graded into personal violence and depredation, destruction of crops, burning of property, and often illegal explusion of the Indians from the vicinity. It was the duty of the resident agents to protect their domains from such insult and damage, but these functionaries lacked the means and authority, and they were often intimidated by threats of reprisal, or even secretly shared the universal animosity against Indians on and off the reservation.

The agents themselves were of inferior grade. The press of the 1850's is replete with such and so many charges against them that credibility is strained. They were incessantly accused of neglecting their duties, of gross immorality, of financial peculations of all sorts, and actually of the murder of those who were placed under their jurisdiction. It is true that a good deal of this controversy was referable to what appears to have been jealousy on the part of the army, the commanding echelon of which was strongly antagonistic to the authority vested in a civilian branch of the government, the Office of Indian Affairs. However, the weight of accusation was very great and by no means without basis. There are too many specific accounts extant, with names, dates, and details. Among these are the writings of J. Ross Browne, a man who espoused the cause of the Indians throughout the period, and who carried considerable influence in Washington and other eastern centers. He attacked T. J. Henley, who may have been as vicious and corrupt an agent as Browne said he was. The verbal struggle between the two men reached such intensity that the Secretary of the Treasury sent out a special investigator to examine the situation. His report, which is still preserved in the National Archive,[8] corroborated most of Browne's charges and put Henley in a very bad light indeed.

In spite of inefficiency, corruption, robbery, and murder, the reservations somehow survived and are still in operation, in effect if not in name. Meanwhile, the Indian population has more or less taken care of itself. Some families managed to weather the hard times of the 1850's and 1860's and remained permanently on reservations, notably Hupa, Round Valley, Tule River, and the small southern units attached to the Mission Agency. Many others simply retreated to the most inaccessible spots they could find. The coastal groups tended to congregate in little rancherias near the abandoned missions, or to settle on ranches in the hills and deserts. The remnants of the northern and Sierra

Nevada tribelets scattered along remote watercourses in the highlands, such as the upper Feather River, the upper San Joaquin, or Stony Creek in Colusa County, where they have lived in relative peace and quiet for over a century. To live, they have carried on small subsistence farms, have taken what jobs they could get, and for the rest have depended upon government relief. An unknown number of others have drifted to the towns and cities, married members of other races, and have lost their identity as aboriginal Californians. Thus the reservations as such have carried only a fraction of the load.

Anglo-American society did not divest itself completely of consideration for the surviving natives, when these were gathered on reservations or otherwise relegated to obscurity and neglect. After a period of quiescence lasting about thirty years, the "Indian question" again attracted public attention in California. The immediate inspiration was the appearance of two books by Helen Hunt Jackson, *The Century of Dishonor,* in 1881, and *Ramona,* in 1884, together with the consequent foundation of the Indian Rights Association. Public sentiment was aroused by these expositions of the sad state in which the southern California Indians were existing. It must also be pointed out that, with the exception of a few die-hard Apache in the Southwest, there were no tribes in a position to offer serious opposition to the Americans. Moreover, as the agitation for unrestricted massacre or mass exile lost force, there arose a feeling of guilt and a recognition of responsibility for the unjust treatment that the Indian had received in the past. One of the results of this shift in attitude was a series of long overdue reforms in the Office of Indian Affairs. One of them authorized purchase by the government of numerous small farms, which were then allotted to heads of families for their support. These allotments were inheritable and could even be sold with permission of the Indian Service.

A protracted series of discussions and hearings before Congressional committees culminated in the passage of the Indian Claims Commission Act of 1946. According to its provisions, any Indian tribe might bring suit for damages inflicted upon the tribe by the American people during the preceding two centuries. The understanding was also clear that once all the claims under the Act had been filed, heard, and adjudicated, there would be no further Indian claims recognized by the United States. The California Indians brought such a suit, based largely upon the promises contained in the treaty of Guadalupe Hidalgo. Extended testimony was taken in Berkeley in 1954, and in San Francisco in 1955. The result has been an award of something over thirty million dollars, the distribution of which is now about to be undertaken. Thus, after one hundred and twenty years, the American people have in some measure compensated the first owners of California for the hardships that they were forced to endure.

Chapter III

Continuities and Discontinuities in Spanish-Speaking California

Moses Rischin

One of the least understood events in California history is the decline of the Spanish-speaking peoples of the pre-1846 period. The United States conquest and subsequent horde of gold-seekers overwhelmed the Hispanic institutions of northern California. South of Monterey, Spanish-speaking people retained considerable influence for more than a decade after the conquest, but the disintegration of the ranchos and the arrival of railroads eventually caused the disappearance of the old order in this part of the state as well. This "decline of the Californios," as Leonard Pitt has called it, was not so much a reduction in physical numbers as a decline in the power, wealth, and cultural identification of a significant ethnic group in California history.

In this chapter, Dr. Moses Rischin discusses the fate of the Californios and the discontinuity which exists between the Spanish-speaking population of Old California and the Mexican and Mexican-American population of the present day. In the development of his theme, Dr. Rischin first discusses the way in which Westerners have perceived the role of immigration and ethnic minorities in their history and then provides a critique of Western historiography itself. Dr. Rischin is Professor of History at San Francisco State College. Among his published works are *The Promised City, "Our Own Kind": Voting by Race, Creed, or National Origin,* and *The American Gospel of Success.*

Continuities and Discontinuities in Spanish-Speaking California

In this discussion, I would like to counterpoint the continuities and discontinuities of the American past, or the past in California, and then look specifically at the position of those in California who were at one time or still are Spanish-speaking. I do this with the feeling that much of American history remains to be written and that every generation writes history to a great extent from the perspective of its own problems. First, I would like to indicate what have been the serious limitations in the writing of the history of the American West in relation to the story of the diverse populations that came to settle it. Then I will speak in particular about the minority group that has been most traditionally associated with California, the Spanish-speaking.

Since 1945, American historians have been hastening to overtake a world-centered United States. Seeking an audience in the world as well as among captive students, they no longer view their nation as an innocent adolescent engaged in a transatlantic feud with an authoritarian European parent. Increasingly, the United States has become a premier trustee and guarantor of civilization, burdened with all the ironies and ambiguities that accompany this new condition. Looking outward, inevitably the nation's historians have come to look inward, and a new cosmopolitanism has gradually been harnessed to the rethinking and rewriting of American social history.[1]

Nowhere is the hiatus between the older history and the new more challenging and more likely to jar than west of the Rockies in the thirteen latter-day original states that now include Alaska and Hawaii, the much-touted "racially aloha" laboratory of democracy. No aspect of the history of the West is more crucial to American self-understanding or more universal in interest than

the virtually unexplored history of the accommodation and inter-
action of its diverse peoples with one another and the implication
of their severance or perpetuation of group or personal ties with
their places of origin in the United States or abroad. No other
region in the United States has seen from its beginning so great
and so varied a mingling of peoples. Nowhere has the need for a
sense of history and identity been more nakedly and critically
felt. Yet, for most Americans, the West has only recently become
a palpable social reality. For them its history in many critical
aspects began to become meaningful only after the closing of the
frontier, when, ironically, all histories of the West end. In 1890,
this region as yet contained only five per cent of the country's
population spread over nearly 40 per cent of its land area. To the
historian east of the Rockies, with a few notable exceptions, the
West, except at the level of gold prospecting and geopolitics, was
a distant backwater as remote from the central concerns of America as was Australia from Great Britain.

The history of the far western region is a history of exceptionalism. Not only has it been recent and contemporary even by
the standards of the new nations, but also its place in American
history has been so stylized and parochialized that it has come to
represent the ultimate in American historical discontinuity. The
myth of the American West increasingly came to provide psy-
chological and inspirational relief from the compelling dilemmas
of a growingly complex society profoundly at odds with its in-
dividualistic agrarian democratic traditions. For those vainly re-
sisting the dissolution of an older American way of life, the Far
West offered a retreat and panacea. There cowboys, Indians, out-
laws, buffalo, prospectors, and other children of nature countered
the discontents of civilization. Given the hyper-American extreme exceptionalist role the Western region was to play, no
understanding of the continuities with the American non-West
or with American civilization or Western European civilization
could be expected to arise. Western historians were yea-sayers,
thrice-over. Both spatially and chronologically, the West was
quite removed from the European civilization that traditionally

served as the foil for the writing and the interpretation of the American story. As a result, the West has borne the glory and the burden of a triple myth—the American, the Western, and finally, the New Western—and its history has inevitably been one-sided.

The foreign immigration story, in every respect the antithesis of the "true American" or "true Western" story, inevitably fell victim to amnesia. Of course, the very subject of immigration has been central, indeed obsessive, to Western history. It has produced some of its most distinguished imaginative and historical writing. But scholarship and veneration have been limited to the pioneer years. In so many books on the West, and on California in particular, one looks up "immigration" in the index only to find that the typical reference is to Orientals and Okies. And that comprises the "immigration story": In no other region of the United States has the term "immigration" (except when applied to Asians) almost exclusively connoted internal native American land migration. Perhaps this is related to the fact that in no other region did the early settlers seek so avidly and so desperately to "quick freeze" the pioneer era into a super-American past, and this is most especially true in California where "the West has come to a focus," as Earl Pomeroy has put it.[2] Probably no other region shifted more abruptly from the heroic pioneer years to the statistical drift years, from Manifest Destiny to the Great Barbecue. Yet, no other region's total history is so overwhelmingly contemporary, falling just below the horizon of living memory, or so relevant and instructive for an understanding of the present.

The very rapidity and intensity of change in the New West —a region so vast, with a population so new and so elusive, so mobile and so diverse, so contemptuous of antecedents and yet so hungry for a past—has made it difficult for the historian to find his bearings. The analytical intelligence that is a hallmark of outstanding historians of stabler and older regions has been noticeably deficient here. Easterners and Far Easterners, Southwesterners and Midwesterners, European immigrants and their sons, transmigrants and those from south of the border as well as north, have swarmed over virgin, unchartered land, sociologically speaking. "Middletown," "Yankee City," "Southern Town," and "Jonesville" have not been matched by a major study of "Western City," for sociologists have been as delinquent as historians. Less ambitious studies of Western communities have been few, except, ironically, for studies of Japanese relocation centers, utopian colonies, and, of course, Indian villages, which have never been in sufficient supply to please the anthropologists. Even Carey McWilliams, who popularized the cause of the nation's minorities in a series of books based on the California scene,[3] came up with a truncated story, for his concerns were too immediately programmatic and his historical research too perfunctory to allow for depth or balance. And McWilliams unfortunately has had no counterpart among professional Western or California historians, invariably strangers themselves to the West, themselves wedded to the Western myth. What Rowland Berthoff has recently written of the Pennsylvania anthracite region in the nineteenth century is not without application both to Far Western society and to its historians: "The story is of groups, classes, institutions, and individuals so equivocally related as to be mutually unintelligible and quite heedless of each other. The region had plenty of groups, classes, institutions, and notable personages to be sure, but it is hard to find among them any functional design of reciprocal rights and duties, and the nuts and bolts which pin together a stable social order."[4]

Even John Hicks, whose comments in the early 1930's on the cosmopolitan sources of culture in the Middle West[5] revealed keen insight and a sense of historical complexity, failed to renew his interest upon crossing the Great Divide. Although he objected to what he regarded as the "parochial Hispanophilia" that prevailed in Berkeley on his arrival, he offered no alternative conception. In 1945, shortly after coming to California, Professor Hicks saluted San Francisco, the site of the founding of the United Nations and the true gateway to the Orient and to Latin America. But, curiously, he ignored that immigrant city's proverbial boast that it harbored the spirit of every land, that provincialism alone was a stranger within the Golden Gate. Today, some twenty years later, the San Francisco Public Library does not maintain a single foreign language newspaper file, although some thirty-odd foreign language and ethnic weeklies are currently published in the Bay area. The fiction has been maintained that the earthquake and fire of 1906 destroyed most of the early newspaper files of this historic, spiritual, and cultural metropolis of the West, although investigation has revealed that the file of San Francisco's oldest Italian newspaper, founded in 1859, was extant in North Beach until recently. And the files of other important newspapers are still precariously lodged in private hands. Needless to say, the city of the Golden Gate is representative, not exceptional, in its indifference until now to the ethnic and social complexities of its own past.

Oblivious to the possibilities of research in social history, Far Western historians have repeatedly taken the casual impressions of a curious trio for chapter and verse. The tendency to cite the tourist, James Bryce,[6] the displaced person, Henry George,[7] and the exile, Josiah Royce,[8] to document the greater Americanization of European immigrants in the West has tended to conceal the vigorous nativism that flourished in the region from its inception and the equally vigorous continuity of diversities. The conspicuously immigrant background of many of the leaders of Far Western nativism has also contributed to a remarkable insensitivity on the part of historians to the extreme conformist pressures which prevailed. It is hardly surprising that the American Indian, Father James Bouchard, upon coming to San Francisco in the 1880's, prudently camouflaged his origins and proceeded to lash out at the Chinese with the vigor and abandon of a second-generation American. The candid Yankee authors of San Francisco's earliest history, published in 1854, minced no phrases in their commitment to an Anglo-Saxon manifest destiny:

> Both the French and German races have played a prominent part in the industrial history of San Francisco and that of California generally. Their numbers are very large in the various min-

ing districts while as we can see they form a considerable proportion of the population of the city. They are not the dominant spirits
of the place for these are of the true American type that ever cry
go ahead. But, they help to execute what the national lords of the
soil, the restless and perhaps unhappy people of progress contrive.
The character of a man may at least partially be inferred from his
"drinks." The true Germans dote on *lager beer* and they are a
heavy, phlegmatic, unambitious race; the French love wines and
they are as sparkling yet without strength or force of character: the
genuine Yankee must have a burning spirit in his multitudinous
drafts. And he is a giant when he begins to work, tearing and
trampling over the *impossibilities* of other races and binding them
to his absolute, insolent will.[9]

Yet nearly half a century later, Josiah Royce, although in-
sisting on the indifference of the Californians to family tradition, avowed that in childhood even he had appreciated three
types of hereditary distinctions in addition to his own—the Chinese, the Mexican, and the Irish. Most Westerners, however,
conceded Royce, were more catholic in their prejudices, showing
a hearty American contempt for things and institutions and people that were stubbornly foreign. Even the statue contributed to
the Hall of Statuary in the Capitol in Washington in 1934 trans-
formed California's patron saint, Junípero Serra, into a tall lean
Westerner conforming to the code of the dime western. By contrast, Douglas Tilden's sculpture of 1908, given by James D.
Phelan to San Francisco's Golden Gate Park, realistically por-
trays a smallish, plump Franciscan. Earl Pomeroy, in the first
major synthesis of Western history, *The Pacific Slope*,[10] devoted
only three pages to the European ethnics, reserving his landmark
discussion for the region's conspicuously different and naked
victims of barbaric violence, not to speak of prejudice, the Orientals and the Mexicans.

Clearly, in the Far West more than in other regions, the
dynamics of group life have remained unexplored and poorly understood, indeed as invisible in works of formal history as they
have been visible in life. California history is written as native

American history, pure and simple. It is not a history which explores the region's continuities and similarities with other regions of America, and it virtually ignores the region's relationships with other countries.

This blind spot in Western history and in California history is not difficult to understand, for it is simply the extreme extension of a traditional American exceptionalism. Presumably, in an area distant from the old, corrupt America and the even older, more corrupt Europe, the troublesome provincialisms of race, religion, region, and nationality that divided and redivided Europe and nearly destroyed the United States could be happily forgotten. The New West's anxiety to bring order out of chaos, its passion to establish its own regional identity *vis à vis* the East, and its avidity for cultural unity were both commendable and understandable. Perhaps it would be best to ignore the immediate past of the immigrants from all the states and all the migrating countries so that they might all the more readily become Americans and Golden Westerners. Indeed, a region and a people without a history seemingly might best select a new identity by claiming a legendary and unique past for itself. The vigorous appeal of such a prospect in California is suggested by the founding in 1850 of the Society of California Pioneers, followed two decades later by organizations such as the Native Sons of the Golden West, the Native Daughters of the Golden West, the California Historical Society, and the Southern California Historical Society, not to speak of E. Clampus Vitus, and culminating at the turn of the century in the Bancroft Library, topped by the Bolton Interfaith Cathedral to a *Nuevo Mundo*.

Indeed, for New Westerners, a self-conscious regionalism virtually became psychologically mandatory in the early years of the twentieth century. And, like other American regionalisms, it found its historian trumpeters of a regional declaration of cultural independence. The Spanish and Hispanic past, however remote and quixotic these periods may appear to contemporaries, Mexican and Anglo alike, provided in the late nineteenth century not only a plausible claim to uniqueness but also a mystique and a golden age, at a time shortly after nineteenth-century extreme individualist Anglo-Saxondom had overwhelmed a communally-oriented caballero culture and had rendered most Californios quixotic and picturesque. Historian Herbert Bolton and his Hispanophile colleagues, who dominated the Western academic empire, inevitably seized upon a cultural pseudo-identity that found sanction in the popular mind even as it lent romance and a common denominator to the researches of diverse rootless scholars, who were isolated physically and professionally from the American mainland. For them, Bolton reassuringly projected a greater American synthesis in the tradition of nineteenth-century historian Francis Parkman, "to Parkmanize," as he romantically put it, the history of the Spanish settlements without incorporating Parkman's anti-Catholicism. To Catholic historians, at odds with the secular and Protestant cultural and intellectual climate of the nineteenth century, Bolton's romance with the Spanish borderlands proved inviting, promoted scholarly good fellowship, and seemed to redress the historic American anti-Catholic prejudice while buttressing and giving respectability to an American Catholic identity and avoiding the unpleasantnesses of the nineteenth century. "The American story need no longer be an unrelieved and in that measure, an unhistorical, Anglo record," is the way one of Bolton's leading Catholic students, Professor John Francis Bannon, recently summed up the virtues of the Bolton School.[11] In *Spanish Arcadia,* a more romantic popular disciple of Bolton's was to rhapsodize on the California West:

> What a contrast there is between the characters of the first settlers on the opposite coasts of our country, almost as though climate had something to do with it. We see landing on the stern and rockbound shore of the stormy Atlantic, the solemn visaged Puritans then seeking to merit heaven while making earth a hell. While to the delightsome land of California, as some of the earliest discoverers term it, came these wanderers from old Castile seeking to make of this world a paradise, singing and dancing their happy lives away on the edge of the peaceful sea.[12]

Bolton's famous course, "The History of the Americas," was auspiciously inaugurated in 1920, a period of American backlash against Europe. Bolton's syllabus made a clear break with older American history no less than with European history, doing so beneath a banner of wider American horizons by a commitment to wider hemispheric isolationism. Indeed, until the coming of Frederick L. Paxson from Wisconsin in 1932, the Berkeley History Department uniquely boasted three American—not United States—historians, Charles E. Chapman, Herbert E. Priestly, and Bolton himself. Eugene McCormick alone professed an isolated United States history. But Paxson's doctoral dissertation, published in 1903, was entitled *The Independence of the South American Republics,* so that even that United States historian (a successor to Frederick Jackson Turner of Wisconsin, the great historian of the frontier) fitted at least sentimentally within Bolton's American-Berkeley school.

To a later generation, that is, to this generation, the cross, sword, and gold pan school of history can only seem eccentric and escapist, a higher provincialism gilding a contemporary isolationism. "The Spanish colony of upper California was virtually without significance until it was annexed by the United States of America," asserted John Hawgood, England's authority on the American West in the Thirteenth Montague-Burton International Relations Lecture.[13] Bolton, said John Higham, more recently, "gave a specious appearance of significance to a program of fragmentary research."[14] Indeed, even Bolton's leading disciples have reluctantly conceded in the last few years that their mentor's focus on colonial history no longer seems relevant.

Yet, if Bolton contributed little that has enlarged the historical understanding of the United States, there is no denying that he sang to the hearts of thousands of students, undergraduates and graduates alike, who found regional and pan-American fellowship in an arcane yet benign hemispheric past that gave the New American West a claim to cultural parity with, if not superiority to, the older regions. Indeed, Professor Bolton's Berkeley following reflected an extreme adulation that is unparalleled in academic life.

Now that we have some perspective on American social, ethnic, and immigration history as it has revealed itself in the literature virtually until this very day, let us turn to a discussion of what I shall call the continuities and discontinuities in Spanish-speaking California with, I trust, a greater degree of insight.

First, I am not sure whether I should speak of the "Spanish story" or the "Mexican story." It is an old, old problem and its solution is still a very uncertain one. The word "Spanish" in Mexican history excites as positive a response as the word "Tory" did in the minds of American patriots of the early nineteenth century. But if you will permit me an occasional gaucherie, what I would like to look at is the actual story of the Spanish Southwest, particularly California, to some extent historically and to an even greater extent in terms of contemporary developments.

Let it be said for the record that although the area of the Spanish Southwest was settled originally by Indians and then by Spaniards, the total number of people settling in California of Spanish or Mexican origin was always very small. California was the most remote region in the Spanish empire, and it remained isolated within the later Mexican republic as well. It was not physically contiguous to Mexico as were New Mexico and the more immediate regions of the Southwest, so that its story has very little of the glamour that one associates with the Spanish Southwest, which came into existence during the golden age of Spanish culture. In those years, Spain was a great imperial power with a culture of great significance. But in the late eighteenth century, the relatively small number of Californios (as they called themselves) had no direct contact with Spain, past or present. In fact, they had very little contact with anyone outside California, having become isolated in a provincial pocket. When Americans in relatively small numbers came in, shortly before the Gold Rush, there was a fairly easy accommodation on both sides. Because the numbers were small, the whole question of American rule did not arise.

Within a generation of the Gold Rush, however, the Californio virtually became extinct—not physically or individually extinct, but extinct as a member of a group with a culture and a language and institutions that could perpetuate themselves. The Californios of nineteenth-century California were very hard put to maintain continuity other than continuity of person. An excellent recent book, *The Decline of the Californios,*[15] is in reality an epitaph to them. This relatively small group, estimated at 15,000 in the 1850's and 1860's, was soon to be submerged by waves of Europeans and Americans just as the Native Sons and Native Daughters of the Golden West have been engulfed by the immigration to California in the last generation. A few years ago, I spoke with a Native Son of the Golden West living in San Diego, who confided that he felt like a Yahoo in his own home, a stranger whose claim that he was born in California in the year 1900 excites the same sort of admiration that is excited by the discovery of other archeological evidences of previous cultures. I imagine that this man could very well empathize with the Californios of the 1850's and 1860's who simply could not in any way come to terms with the massive changes that were transforming a pastoral California into an agricultural California.

In fact, to speak of Spanish continuities and discontinuities in Spanish-speaking California is in reality to speak mostly of discontinuities. I think that if there is a continuity, it is primarily sentimental. It is not a physical continuity in which institutions or people maintain themselves, or which allows for a resolution of the problems of identity of the Spanish-speaking Californian. It is perhaps conceivable that the Californio culture could have been sustained, in the same way that the cultures of European immigrants have been sustained, if the Californio culture had not been virtually illiterate. Spanish-language newspapers existed for the briefest periods of time. The longest-lived newspaper, *El Clamor Publico,* lasted for four years in the 1850's, a time when there were dozens of French, Italian, German, and other newspapers coming into being not only in San Francisco and the Bay area but in the West as a whole. Even if other circumstances had been ideal, it is unlikely that continuity could have been maintained with such a lack of communication.

The great migration to the Southwest from Mexico began in the early years of the twentieth century, continuing with ever-increasing momentum in subsequent decades to a point where there are now perhaps five or six million people who have been designated as Spanish-speaking in the Southwest and eight million in the United States as a whole. Yet there is, at best, but a tenuous relationship between this Hispanic world and Herbert Bolton's pre-1776 Hispanic world or the later world of the Californios. The persistence of Spanish names for our streets, towns, and cities may be satisfying to people of Spanish-speaking origin. In more vital respects, however, there has been a dearth, if not a total absence, of established groups to which Mexicans have been able to turn. Even the Catholic Church, which might have been considered a sort of residuary legatee, was overwhelmed by a population strange in language and culture in an area that was in so many ways undermanned and desperately in need of clergymen, schools, and other institutions.

Under such conditions, Mexicans have been relatively isolated in twentieth-century California. They found themselves with no natural bridges of access to the larger American society. As other immigrants were becoming Americanized and becoming Anglos, the Mexicans seemed more isolated than ever.

The industrial underdevelopment of the Southwest and California also meant that for a long time there would be no pressure for great change on the Mexicans coming into these areas. They could come to the southwestern United States without making any radical alterations in their life patterns. Unlike most immigrants, they did not cross the Atlantic or Pacific, but simply passed over the border and entered into an agricultural world resembling that of their own country, a country to which they could always return with relative ease.

Given these conditions, a cultural stalemate ensued. Indeed, some students of Spanish America have tended to view the Spanish-speaking as a group at an opposite pole from the larger American society, as a group with entirely contrasting value clusters. The Anglo world's dominant value is the value of order, while the Hispano world's dominant value is the value of anarchism. Anarchism, of course, can be defined positively as individuality, vitality, passion, integrity, freedom. It can also be defined negatively as chaos, inefficiency, crime, and violence. Order, in the same way, can be viewed positively as efficiency, progress, cleanliness, stability, justice. It can also be viewed negatively as sterile, antiseptic, timid, rigid, and innocuous. Clearly, most Americans are identified as Anglos, while the Mexicans identify themselves as something apart, as Chicanos. California, machine-like in its order and rationalized to an extreme, only further accentuates the sense of cultural impasse.

The confrontation between Anglos and Mexicans leaves few options. Either one becomes an Anglo or one remains a Mexican. A real option is open only to the relatively few, while the rest drop out. The entry key to the Anglo world in the twentieth century has been the educational system, to which the Mexican-American of rural folk origin finds himself little able to adapt. The values of his primordial ethnicity (and I do not mean his ideology) make it apparent that the American gospel of success is not for him. Mexican-American schoolboys do not realize that their culture emphasizes "being" rather than "doing" or "becoming." But by failing or dropping out of the school system— the Spanish-speaking have the highest drop-out rate by far—the Mexican-American boy rejects the culture entirely, or perhaps reverts back to the most extreme expression of his own culture.

As the Mexican-American looks upon the scene about him, it becomes quite clear that the world upon which he is entering is completely at opposite poles from the one from which he comes, and that a middle ground is virtually non-existent. It is significant that relatively few Mexican-Americans who have made it into the Anglo world have retained a Spanish-speaking identity. Those who have made it have done so presumably at the price of cutting themselves off from their origins.

The world as the school represents it to the Mexican-American certainly has not been represented effectively. Although the Spanish culture from which the Spanish-speaking come verges on the illiterate, in the last few years there has been a 95 per cent penetration of this population by television. Suddenly entering on the scene has been a force that, for better or worse, has come to dominate an area of culture, serving a purpose which the school has found very difficult to combat. In many ways, television is the very obverse of the school, with its emphasis on hard learning. If the struggle between open-ended television and the classroom is sensed in the homes of Americans who are monocultural, then one can very well imagine what it must be like for people who have never experienced the classroom in any way. They reject it entirely in favor of the friendly television world, where they find much in the way of Spanish-language broadcasting, much that is familiar, and much that is easy to accept because it makes little demand on the viewer. Despite the long history of American immigration and cultural diversity, American educators have never been able really to translate cultural differences in a positive way. No classroom has ever been as congenial as contemporary foreign-language television, however inane. American education has been fundamentally middle class both at its best and at its worst, and it has been fundamentally monolithic. What then becomes of Mexican-American youngsters?

Students of the Mexican-Americans have envisaged three possibilities for the future of the group in America. The first is the prevailing *co-existence,* where contacts remain institutional, are minimal, and never become direct. The second, practiced less conspicuously perhaps, has been *assimilation,* beginning through the exercise of the rights of equal educational and employment opportunities, and continuing through the acceptance by Mexican-Americans of the small family pattern, the employment of women outside the home, and guidance by psychiatrists rather than by priests. The final option and the most promising one—if not in terms of possibilities, then at least in terms of ideals—is a kind of *synthesis* of cultures that would make possible a personal integration and self-direction rooted in the Hispanic character traits of Mexican-Americans but dovetailing with the orderliness and efficiency associated with the Anglos. The result might well be a healthy schizophrenia.[16]

Selected Questions and Answers

Q. "Why are we branded with the name 'Mexican-American'? Why aren't European and Middle Eastern immigrants called 'Russian-Americans,' 'Turkish-Americans,' 'Arab-Americans'? A Mexican is always a branded American, yet he has been here much longer than any immigrant from Europe."

A. "This is a curious situation. During the great age of immigration to America in the nineteenth and early twentieth centuries, such hyphenate designations were commonplace. If you look at the biography of Joseph P. Kennedy, the father of John and Robert Kennedy, you will note that although he was a Harvard graduate and an extremely successful banker, he constantly resented the fact that people identified him as an Irish-American. I think it is inevitable that there should be great sensitivity on this score because it seems to suggest inferiority."

Q. "I'm proud of being Mexican."

A. "What happened in the nineteenth century was that the early settlers here who were of Mexican origin began to call themselves 'Californios' or 'Hispanos' so that people wouldn't confuse them with the new Mexicans. This is very common in the history of immigration—an attempt in some way by an earlier group to cast off any kind of identification with a newer group analogous or identical with itself for fear of suffering some sort of discrimination. As I have emphasized, discrimination and nativism have been deeply rooted in the American past, given the great diversity of people who have come to America. It's true that it still persists, and it persists with respect to the newer comers. But I think it persists with less intensity than it did in the nineteenth and early twentieth centuries. The contacts of dissimilar cultures often tend to be hostile rather than fraternal. They can be one or the other, but it takes a great deal of effort to build a fraternal rather than a hostile world."

Q. "Most of the problems you mentioned of isolation and discrimination in the schools have been faced by all immigrants. The problem of losing your old culture and becoming American has also been an old one. Many Mexican-Americans are fourth- or fifth-generation immigrants. Are they finding it a little harder to drop their sub-culture because they are so close to Mexico?"

A. "Yes, I think that there are two groups in the United States who have migrated in very large numbers who are relatively close to their places of origin, and for them a break with their past is difficult. From north of the border, French Canada has sent great numbers of French Canadians to New England and to the border states all the way from New York to Minnesota. From south of the border, from Mexico, people move freely, at least relatively freely, into the Southwest without much expense or effort. The result, of course, is an enduring sense of continuity which is rare for third- or fourth-generation Americans coming from Europe or from Asia."

Chapter IV

Strangers in the Cities: The Chinese on the Urban Frontier

Stanford M. Lyman

Anti-Orientalism is one of the most persistent themes in California history. From the arrival of Chinese workers in the gold fields during the 1850's to the forced relocation of people of Japanese descent during World War II, California life was marked by open, organized, and sometimes violent discrimination against Orientals. Since the war, most of this prejudice has disappeared from the surface of California society, an event which warrants more study than it has received thus far. However, beneath the surface, the stereotypes and fears first formulated in the 1850's may still affect California life more than we like to admit.

In this chapter, Dr. Stanford M. Lyman discusses the historical experience of California's urban Chinese population. Dr. Lyman not only deals with the tradition of anti-Orientalism, but also covers the history and complex internal structure of the Chinese community itself. Dr. Lyman is Professor of Sociology at the University of Nevada and former Chairman of the Department of Anthropology and Sociology at Sonoma State College. He is the author of many articles and has served as consultant to several California school districts in the development of curricula in minority studies.

Strangers in the Cities:
The Chinese
on the Urban Frontier

To speak of the Chinese in San Francisco—and, for that matter, in Seattle, Vancouver, New York City, and other large cities—as *strangers* is to describe them in terms first enunciated by the great sociologist Georg Simmel. "The stranger," wrote Simmel in his essay of that title, "is ... not ... the wanderer who comes today and goes tomorrow, but rather is the person who comes today and stays tomorrow."[1] The Chinese immigrants in America, and in the other areas to which they had journeyed, were characterized by their self-imposed status as sojourners.[2] They were, as Simmel observed of strangers in general, potential wanderers, but not persons without fixed places to go. Rather they went in the first instance to those places where opportunity beckoned, and ultimately they would return to the original homeland which called them back from their diaspora and invited them to the warmth of hearth and domesticity. While abroad they were geographically near but socially distant from the peoples in the host societies. They were *in* the host society but not *of* it. They had not belonged to the host society from the beginning and they imported things—culture, ways of life, ideas—into it which it had not contained previously and which would not, in the ordinary course of events, have arisen among the host society's people autochthonously.

As strangers the Chinese aroused interest, curiosity, and hostility. From the first, their presence generated ideas about them. But there was a difference between generated interest and curiosity, and knowledgeable ideas. The pictures of the Chinese that emerged in the American mind were stereotypes, categorical images of human objects, built up around shreds and patches of

[63]

thoughts and notions about China and supplemented by cursory observations unilluminated by any profound cultural, social, or historical intelligence.[3] Reinforced by reiteration and legitimized through enunciation by social and political elites, these stereotypes laid the basis for legislative hostilities and popular uprisings against the Chinese, and these in turn strengthened the original pejorative imagery. Only after the Chinese population had declined considerably and had accommodated itself to a ghetto existence within the urban structure, and when other racial and ethnic groups seemed more threatening, did the hostility against the Chinese die down. The stereotypes did not disappear but instead took on a benign form, couched in patronizing and indulgent terms. They are still employed as both symbol and artifice in the maintenance of social distance.

Chinese Immigration to America

American interest in China antedates immigration from that nation by more than half a century. The *Chinoiserie* movement[4] which swept over Europe from the sixteenth through the eighteenth century left its mark on America, where Chinese bric-a-brac was to be found in colonial and frontier homes well into the nineteenth century,[5] and where Chinese art collections began early to become prized possessions of both private persons and museums.[6] Several magnificent houses were built in the "Chinese style" in colonial America, and Chinese tapestries adorned many a wall of American gentlemen and traders.[7] Indeed, one of the compelling economic reasons for the American Revolution was the desire of American merchants and traders to wrest control of the China trade from British domination. China's importance to the new republic was symbolized by the early appointment of Major Samuel Shaw as Consul at Canton in 1786, the first American consulate beyond the Cape of Good Hope.[8]

However, interest in China's art, architecture, and government was not accompanied by very much knowledge of, or deep compassion for, the Chinese people. To be sure, the Jesuits in sixteenth-century Peking had exaggerated an image of efficient public administration and lack of military aggression in China which had impressed Europeans and some Americans.[9] But these ideas were not spread far and wide in America; rather there was general indifference about the Chinese people, and occasional approval of China's policy of isolation from foreign influence.[10] From 1787 until 1848, very few Chinese visited the United States. A Chinese colony, settled in Nootka Sound in 1788, lasted only until 1789, and some other Chinese brought to the northwest coast of America travelled on ships along the entire Pacific coast until around 1791, a few deserting in Mexico.[11] An earlier Chinese settlement in Mexico City in 1635 had come to naught as well.[12] A few Chinese seamen had been temporarily abandoned in Pennsylvania in 1785–1786, while others occasionally worked as sailors on the New England ships that engaged in the China trade, even though an American law of 1817 limited foreign sailors on American ships to no more than one-third of the crew —one Chinese cook shipped as "George Harrison of Charlestown, Mass."[13] In 1809, John Jacob Astor had persuaded President Jefferson to exempt his ship from the embargo on China then in force by representing one of his Chinese crew members as an important mandarin who had to be returned to his native land;[14] four years later the American ship *Sally* docked in Plymouth with a Chinese passenger who, in full mandarin regalia, attended the Sabbath meeting the following Sunday.[15] In 1830, John P. Cushing, one of the most influential merchants in the China trade, retired with a retinue of Chinese servants.[16]

The education of Chinese in America had interested some Americans. In 1800, James Magee brought a Chinese over to learn English.[17] In 1818, a school for foreign students at Cornwall, Connecticut—begun for the purpose of "education in our own country of Heathen youth, in such manner, as with subsequent professional instruction, will qualify them to become useful Missionaries, Physicians, Surgeons, School Masters or interpreters, and to communicate to the Heathen Nations such knowledge in agriculture and the arts as may prove the means of promoting Christianity and civilization"[18]—admitted the first of five Chinese students. Their history at the school, as well as the denouement of the school itself, has been reported by a descendant of one of the school's founders:

> Wong Arce came in 1818 from Canton. He was brought by a New York merchant who had employed him in Canton and was soon dismissed for disobedience and immorality. In 1823 Ah Lan and Ah Lum came from Philadelphia, stayed two years and were also dismissed for misconduct. In 1825 Chop Ah See was in the school for a while. From 1822–25 Lieaou Ah See, known also as William Botelho, came from Boston and is regarded as the first Protestant convert. Lieaou, who was reported as faithful but far from brilliant, is supposed to have died a Christian in China. The boys were supported partly by charity but mainly by manual labor. The school was closed in 1827 because two Cherokee Indians married two prominent white girls in Cornwall. There was no correspondence recorded with the Chinese after their departure from the school and the experiment seems, as far as the Chinese were concerned, to have been a failure.[19]

Forty-five years were to pass before the Chinese government, urged by Yung Wing, who had become America's first Chinese college graduate when he received a degree from Yale University in 1854,[20] would send over one hundred Chinese young men to study in America as part of the ill-fated Chinese Educational Mission. In 1881, concerned over the growing Americanization of these Chinese youth, their popularity with white girls, their neglect and even deprecation of Chinese studies, ethics, and practices (including the wearing of the queue, which they had petitioned their tutor for permission to sever),[21] the Chinese government recalled the entire mission and required that the students return to China.[22]

That Americans regarded Chinese persons with a mixture of curiosity and amazement is indicated in the reactions of some of the early visitors. In 1808, a Chinese equestrian was employed as a stage performer in New York City. A Chinese juggler performed in the same city in 1842.[23] Chinese sailors and their dog, aboard the junk *Ke Ying* docked at Providence in 1847, were nearly as great a curiosity to the Rhode Island visitors as was the ship itself.[24] One year after the junk had left, P. T. Barnum opened his Chinese museum in New York City. Two traits of the Chinese continued to puzzle and astonish Americans throughout the nineteenth century. One was the plaited queue worn by Chinese men, a mark of subjection imposed on them by the Manchu conquerors in 1645. The Chinese queue was a constant source of amusement and derision to Californians, who plagued Chinese immigrants by cutting off or pulling on their "pigtails,"[25] and who in the 1870's attempted to punish Chinese by prohibiting the wearing of this badge of citizenship.[26] The other was the practice among Chinese of binding the feet of their women, a custom so remarkable to Occidentals that as late as 1834 a Chinese woman in traditional dress and with bound feet was exhibited as a freak attraction on Broadway.[27] Although "pigtails" and footbinding were the features of Chinese life most commented upon—not only by Americans but also by other peoples, such as the Japanese, who tried to extirpate the practices when they assumed rule in Taiwan[28]—other traits and customs aroused curiosity, astonishment, or indignation. The fact that they had "yellow" complexions and "slanted" eyes, that Chinese men all wore the same style of clothing (a loose blue blouse, with matching trousers and a broad-brimmed hat), that they regularly remitted money and the corpses of their dead to China, that they spoke an "unintelligible" cacophonous language, that they seemed to adopt only a crude "pidgin" English, that they appeared to gamble incessantly and to be addicted to opium-smoking, that they carried peculiar diseases, and that they came without their wives or sweethearts—each and every one of these real and imagined, alleged and exaggerated, traits contributed to the belief that the Chinese were a strange, exotic, and even a dangerous people.

Chinese immigration to America effectively began in 1847. A coincidence of catastrophe in China and opportunity in California supplied the expulsive and attractive elements that linked the Middle Kingdom to the United States. Political unrest had been a constant feature of life in Kwangtung and Fukien Provinces since the Manchu conquest of 1644.[29] Overpopulation, once considered no problem at all, presented ever-increasing pressures on agricultural production and distribution after 1800.[30] In addition, foreign intrigues by several of the European nations and the United States had seriously encroached upon Chinese sovereignty, arousing an incipient nationalism directed against both the foreigners and the Manchu regime.[31] Then, in 1849, a terrible flood wreaked havoc on the already wretched lives of southeastern China's peasants. "The rains have been falling for forty days," said a memorial to the emperor, "until the rivers, and the seas, and the lakes, and the streams, have joined in one sheet over the land for several hundred *li* [three *lis* are equal to one English mile] and there is no outlet by which the waters may retire."[32] An observer who wrote for *Blackwood's Magazine* noted that, on the basis of missionary reports, "ten thousand people were destroyed, and domestic animals drowned in untold numbers; crowds even of first families were begging bread, and (horror of horrors to the pious Celestials!) coffins were floating about everywhere on the face of the waters . . . . Such an inundation is too stupendous for the European mind adequately to comprehend its extent, and is said to have exceeded any similar disaster within the memory of the present generation."[33] Natural disaster was followed by rebellion and revolution. In 1851, the Taiping revolutionaries raised their standard against the empire in a civil insurrection that would last for fourteen years and result in casualties estimated to be greater than 30,000,000.[34] In the same period, the Cantonese unsuccessfully fought against invasions by British, French, and American mercenary forces, and also against Hakkas invading from the northwest.[35] The stage was set for continuous anti-Manchu rebellions and anti-foreign uprisings.[36] As a result of all these catastrophic and dislocating events, hundreds of thousands of Chinese were uprooted from their villages. Many fled to the coastal seaports of Canton, Hong Kong, and Macao, where they hoped to find work, to secure aid from kinsmen, or to go abroad temporarily until they could recoup their losses and return to loved ones as wealthy men.

Then gold was discovered in California.[37] A few Chinese merchants had already arrived in California, and they sent word back to kinsmen and friends of the remarkable discovery.[38] Meanwhile, shipping lines and independent sea captains, realizing the profits to be made in adding passenger traffic to the brisk commercial trade with China, sailed into southeastern Chinese ports with circulars advertising the gold discovery and offering cheap passage to California.[39] The excitement created by the news, coupled with the fabulous accounts brought back by the first Chinese returnees, started a brisk passenger trade which, while its vicissitudes were many during the period of "free" immigration, did not subside considerably until American law placed restrictive limits on it in 1882.[40]

The method by which most Chinese came to California was a variant of the indenture system which two centuries earlier had brought Englishmen to the colonies[41] and which a few decades later would bring southern and eastern Europeans to work in the burgeoning industries of the Northeast.[42] The "credit-ticket" system, as it has been called,[43] enabled an impoverished Chinese to come across the ocean, find lodging and food in San Francisco, and be assisted to going to work in the mines, on the railroads, or in the Midwest and the East as a strikebreaker, without putting up any cash. Money for his passage was obtained from kinsmen or fellow-villagers, who assigned the collection of the debt to kinsmen or *Landsmänner* in San Francisco. The latter, organized into caravansaries, met the immigrant at the point of debarkation, accompanied him to the hostel in which his compatriots dwelt, and provided him with food, a place to sleep, and a certain amount of protection from anti-Chinese elements. Most important, the merchant leaders of the *hui kuan (Landsmann-schaften)* acted as contractors or sub-contractors and sent out gangs of men to work. The debts incurred by the Chinese immigrants were deducted from their wages by Chinese headmen, and defalcating debtors were prevented from escaping back to China

by special arrangements between the Chinese creditor associations and the merchant fleet. The entire system was fraught with
corruption, and undoubtedly not a few Chinese found themselves
poorer off in the end than they had been when they began their
American adventure, so that many were forced to stay overseas
much longer than they had anticipated.[44]

Although an American law of 1862 forbade the immigration
of involuntary contract labor, the ignorance and corruptibility of
American consuls at Canton and the nefarious methods of Chinese "crimps" combined to effect the illegal traffic in human
flesh.[45] One incident is of particular importance because it
introduced Chinese laborers into the South and indicates the
limited interest held by Americans in the Chinese. Following the
Civil War, there was a severe labor shortage on plantations in
Louisiana, Arkansas, and other states of the defunct Confed-
eracy. This vexing situation eventually resulted in a bizarre
scheme to import Chinese. Originated at the Memphis convention of 1869, subsidized by two major railroads, supported by
newspapers in the North as well as the South, and effected by the
"crimping" activities of the notorious labor contractor Tye Kim
Orr and the mysterious shipmaster Cornelius Koopmanschap,
the "Chinese experiment" resulted in the inveiglement of two
hundred Chinese aboard the ship *Ville de St. Lo* in 1870. Some
jumped overboard when they learned their fate; others bided their
time, and, when the ship deposited its human cargo in New Or-
leans, they ran away.[46] Some of them may have made up the
early Chinese settlements in the South; the others probably migrated into the Midwest, journeyed on to California, or moved
into the industrial Northeast.[47]

The appearance of Chinese in the Midwest and South took
place after the anti-Chinese movement had begun in California.
Riots against the Chinese seem not to have occurred in the former
Confederate states, largely because there the Chinese were not
perceived as a competitive but rather as an exploitable element
in the labor force, often to be used as a club against recalcitrant Negro laborers.[48] In Colorado, however, where Chinese

began to settle in 1870, one of the worst riots ever against the immigrants from the Middle Kingdom took place in Denver on October 31, 1880.[49] It was one of the signals that the Sinophobic virus, once a localized malady, had become a nearly national epidemic.

The Beginnings of the Anti-Chinese Movement

At first there were only a few Chinese in America. Most of them were located in San Francisco, where they acted as purveyors of art goods, foods, and also prefabricated houses, which were floated across the Pacific and reassembled in the city crowded with gold-seekers.[50] During the first few months of their stay in California, the Chinese merchants were regarded as a curious but welcome addition to an already heterogeneous population composed of Mexicans, Indians, Americans, Chileans, Australians, and various Europeans. They participated in civic festivals, thrived in their mercantile establishments, and were expected, as one San Francisco newspaper prophesied, soon to serve in the legislature.[51] "We shall undoubtedly have a very large addition to our population," wrote an editor of the *Daily Alta Californian* on May 12, 1851, "and it may not be many years before the halls of Congress are graced by the presence of a long-queued Mandarin sitting, voting, and speaking beside a don from Santa Fe and a Kanaker from Hawaii . . . . The 'China boys' will yet vote at the same polls, study at the same schools, and bow at the same altar as our own countrymen."

However, this period of welcome, this sense of social toleration and sympathetic response, this recognition of California as a culturally plural society, disappeared very quickly when Chinese began to appear in the gold mines.[52] The gold mines of California and the other states where the precious ore was discovered were never dominated by the Chinese. Indeed, it would appear that they often worked mines that had already been abandoned by white men.[53] Nevertheless, they were attacked rigorously and viciously by both public laws and popular uprisings. California's infamous Foreign Miners' Tax, enacted first in 1850, and then repealed, re-enacted and reset irregularly until it was declared void in 1870, was enforced from the beginning almost exclusively against the Chinese, who paid 50 per cent of the total revenues obtained from it during its first four years and 98 per cent during its final sixteen years of operation.[54] Moreover, beginning in 1852, the California legislature began what would be more than a quarter of a century of vain experimentation with laws designed to restrict or to exclude altogether the coming of Chinese to the state.[55]

In addition to harassing and restrictive legislation, the Chinese were subjected to popular tribunals and mob violence in the mines. In Chinese Camp, as early as 1849, an uprising took place against sixty Chinese miners. At Marysville, in 1852, white miners drew up a resolution asserting that "no Chinaman was to be thenceforth allowed to hold any mining claim in the neighborhood."[56] There followed a general uprising in the area against the Chinese, and, accompanied by a marching band, white miners expelled the Chinese from North Forks, Horseshoe Bar, and other neighboring mining camps.[57] By 1856, the following laws were in operation in California's Columbia mining district: "Neither Asiatics nor South-Sea Islanders shall be allowed to mine in this district, either for themselves or for others." "Any person who shall sell a claim to an Asiatic or a South-Sea Islander shall not be allowed to hold another claim in this district for the space of six months."[58] In New Kanaka Camp, Tuolomne Colony, the Chinese were excluded entirely, "not allowed to own either by purchase or pre-emption."[59] As late as 1882, the laws of Churn Creek District forbade any miner to sell a claim to the Chinese,[60] and Chinese were rarely to be seen in that county. In 1858 and 1859, there were again attempts to expel the Chinese from the placers, and Chinese were routed out of Vallecito, Douglas Flat, Sacramento Bar, Coyote Flat, Sand Flat, Rock Creek, Spring Creek, and Buckeye.[61]

By the end of the decade, gold mining was coming to an end for both Chinese and other pioneers. Gold strikes in British Columbia in 1858 and gold, silver, and copper mining in the Rocky

Mountain area would attract some Chinese for the next thirty years and extend the miners' anti-Chinese movement eastward and also into Canada. However, by the mid 1860's many Chinese were beginning to move into other occupations—railroad building, food, laundry, manufacturing, merchandising, and domestic service—occupations which located them in cities. As the 1850's closed, the Chinese accounted for 25 per cent of California's miners, yet this fact alone, as Rodman W. Paul has pointed out, suggests the decline of the mines.[62] Descriptions of Chinese miners in the 1860's indicate the reduced state of the industry. Writing in the 1860's, an anonymous erstwhile miner described the area around Sonora: "Whole acres of land have been upturned and the earth and sand passed through a second and third washing, and apparently every particle of gold extracted; yet the less ambitious Chinese and Mexicans find enough in these deserted places to reward them for their tedious labors."[63] In Tuolomne County, Chinese worked mines so far below the streams that the ore had to be "packed" up to the water: "Here we see troops of sturdy Chinamen groaning along under the weight of huge sacks of earth brought to the surface from a depth of eighteen feet and deposited in heaps after a weary tramp along the banks of a muddy pool."[64] William H. Brewer, who traveled throughout California in the years 1860–1864, described the town of Weaver as "a *purely* mining town . . . so it is like California in bygone times." There he found a church "sluiced around until only enough land remains for it to stand upon . . . and multitudes of Chinese—the men miners, the women frail, very frail, industrious in their calling." At Eureka: "Ten white men and two Chinamen slept in the little garret of the 'hotel.' Our horses fared but little better, and our bill was the modest little sum of fifteen dollars." Along the Klamath River: "Here and there a poor Chinaman plies his rocker, gleaning gold from sand, once worked over with more profit, but there are few white inhabitants left until we reach Happy Camp."[65]

Despite the decline of the mining industry, or perhaps because of it, Chinese were still expelled from areas in which they had settled down to work or were forcibly driven out of their jobs. A few Chinese were employed in and around some quicksilver mines near Calistoga until 1900; they were indulged as servants so long as they appeared docile and obsequious, but they were as often suspected of thievery and kept under surveillance.[66] The Chinese who had been employed in quartz mining, often "for certain inferior purposes, such as dumping cars, surface excavations, etc.,"[67] were driven out of that occupation in Sutter Creek as a concession to striking white miners in 1871.[68] In 1885, the leading citizens of Eureka ordered the entire Chinese population to leave Humboldt County on one day's notice or suffer the injuries of which an outraged mob was capable. When a few Chinese were brought to the area in 1906, the town again forcibly removed them. As late as 1937, Humboldt County boasted of its riddance of the hated Chinese.[69] The 1880's witnessed the beginning of over two decades of public threats, popular agitation, and prejudiced reporting about the Chinese in Napa County which ended with their decline or departure around the turn of the century.[70] By the end of the nineteenth century, the California Chinese had, for the most part, died off, returned to China, moved eastward, or settled down in those ghettos of American cities referred to as "Chinatowns." They would remain in the latter to the present day.

The mining frontier of the west moved eastward, and with it went some of the Chinese—and after them came nativist movements to remove their tiny colonies or restrict their meager opportunities.[71] Oregon, Idaho, Montana, Nevada, and Wyoming felt a Chinese presence in the last three decades of the nineteenth century. British Columbia and Alaska also at first employed Chinese and then attempted to exclude them in this period. The Chinese entered Oregon in the late 1860's, apparently following after the whites who worked the newly-discovered gold fields in the eastern part of that state. By 1870, mining had declined considerably in Oregon, as was evidenced by the fact that the Chinese numbered 2,428 of the 3,965 miners there.[72] A similar decline in mining in Idaho caused many whites to sell out to Chinese, so that by 1870 more than half the state's miners were Chinese; by 1880, the ratio of Chinese to whites in Idaho was higher than in any state or territory in the Union.[73] Chinese settlement in Montana began at least as early as 1869 and continued to increase irregularly until 1910, after which it declined until in 1940 only 258 were left in Butte, a city which had once complained of over 2,500 Chinese.[74] Nevada had had a small Chinese population by the mid-1850's, a fact testified to by the renaming of the settlement first known as Hall's Station to Chinatown;[75] by the 1870's a thriving Chinese community had been established at Virginia City as a result of the Comstock mining boom, and it was soon the object of curiosity and suspicion.[76] The Chinese community at Rock Springs, Wyoming, was the scene in 1885 of one of the worst riots ever spawned by the anti-Oriental feeling in America.[77] Chinese settlement in British Columbia began with the Fraser River gold strike in 1858, which brought several thousand Chinese from California's sluiced-out fields,[78] and it was increased by the importation of Chinese to build the Canadian Pacific Railroad.[79] The Chinese stay in Alaska was as brutish as it was short. Imported to work the picked-over gold mines of John Treadwell in 1885, they were confronted by angry, demoralized, unemployed white and Indian mine laborers and attacked with dynamite. One year later they were incarcerated and expelled from the territory; after 1886, no more Chinese were employed in Alaskan mines.[80]

The Sinophobia which gripped California spread to the Rocky Mountain area in the wake of the Chinese miners. An editorial in an Arizona newspaper is typical of its genre and reveals both the nature and depth of the hatred against the Chinese:

The Chinese are the least desired immigrants who have ever sought the United States . . . the almond-eyed Mongolian with his pigtail, his heathenism, his filthy habits, his thrift and careful accumulation of savings to be sent back to the flowery kingdom.

The most we can do is to insist that he is a heathen, a devourer of soup made from the fragrant juice of the rat, filthy, disagreeable, and undesirable generally, an incumbrance that we do not know how to get rid of, but whose tribe we have determined shall not increase in this part of the world.[81]

Similar views inflamed the people of other states in the Rockies, occasionally modified by a recognition of the benefits obtained from the Chinese. Thus, in Silver City, Idaho, the *Owyhee Avalanche* asserted, "They are in many respects a disgusting element of the population but not wholly unprofitable."[82] However, more people seemed to agree with the Montana journalist who wrote, "We don't mind hearing of a Chinaman being killed now and then, but it has been coming too thick of late . . . soon there will be a scarcity of Chinese cheap labor in the country . . . Don't kill them unless they deserve it, but when they do—why kill 'em lots."[83] Opposition to the Chinese was not merely a pastime of journalists; Montana Governor James M. Ashley expressed the views of much of the citizenry and many of his fellow governors in the West when he said that his state needed "Norwegians, Swedes, and Germans," not Chinese:

It will be conceded by all practical men who have given this subject any thought, that Montana is better adopted [sic] to the hardy races of men and women from Great Britain and Northern Europe . . . . I am . . . opposed to the importation of laborers from any of the barbarous or semi-civilized races of men, and do not propose to cooperate in any scheme organized to bring such laborers into Montana, or into any part of the country.[84]

By 1880, the drive to exclude Chinese that began in California and moved eastward to the Rockies had spread throughout the nation, and it laid the basis for America's first bill of immigration restriction based on race. In 1870, Chinese laborers had been shipped from California to North Adams, Massachusetts, to break a strike of shoemakers. Hailed at first by those opposed to the striking union, the Knights of St. Crispin, the Chinese were subsequently the objects of anti-coolie meetings held in Boston to protest the reduction of American labor to the standards of "rice and rats."[85] In 1877, another gang of Chinese were imported from California to break a cutlery manufacturing strike in Beaver Falls, Pennsylvania.[86] The *Cincinnati Enquirer* and other Ohio papers protested against the use of Chinese labor in the cigar-making industry,[87] the industry whose union leader, Samuel Gompers, was to become a lifelong foe of the Chinese and one of the most potent forces in denying them an equal opportunity in craft work.[88] America's labor unions fulminated against the Chinese and demanded their exclusion from the nation and their expulsion from the labor force. "The political issue after 1877 was racial, not financial, and the weapon was not merely the ballot, but also 'direct action'—violence. The anti-Chinese agitation in California, culminating as it did in the Exclusion Law passed by Congress in 1882, was doubtless the most important single factor in the history of American labor, for without it the entire country might have been overrun by Mongolian labor and the labor movement might have become a conflict of races instead of one of classes."[89] That a historian of labor, writing in the twentieth century, could make this statement is indicative of the depth to which Sinophobia had worked itself into at least one sector of the American population.

Settlement in Cities

One of the outstanding characteristics of the Chinese in America is their settlement in cities. Unlike the Japanese, for example, the Chinese did not have a long habitation on agricultural hinterlands followed by the migration of second and third generation offspring to urban areas.[90] A few Chinese agricultural settlements had existed briefly in the California interior,[91] and some Chinese farmers are to be found in the rural environs of Vancouver, British Columbia, but the bulk of Chinese have always dwelt in cities or small towns.[92] Even when Chinese were employed on railroads, such as the Central Pacific in the late 1860's, or in digging the tunnels of California's vineyards,[93] their places of work were but temporary abodes; when the work was done they returned to the city. "San Francisco," testified Frank

M. Pixley, politician, publisher, and opponent of Chinese immigration, "is the heart and hive and home of all the Chinese upon this coast. Our Chinese quarter, as it is called, is their place really of residence. If they go to a wash house in the vicinity, to a suburban manufactory, to gardening near the town, or if to build railroads in San Bernardino or on the Colorado, or to reclaim tule lands in the interior, their departure there is temporary, and their return here is certain; therefore the number in San Francisco depends upon seasons and the contract labor market."[94]

The Chinese population of San Francisco grew both in an absolute and a proportional sense in the decades after 1860. In 1860, the Chinese in San Francisco numbered 2,719 persons and were only 7.8 per cent of the state's total Asian population. By 1870, it had jumped to 12,030 and 24.4 per cent; ten years later it had risen to 21,745 and 28.9 per cent; in 1890, the Chinese in San Francisco had grown to 25,833 and 35.7 per cent. Only in 1900 did the number of Chinese in San Francisco show a decline. The enforcement of the exclusion laws, the return of numerous successful or discouraged Chinese to China, and the departure of others for the Midwest and beyond left the number at 13,954, still 30.5 per cent of the state's Chinese population.[95]

The city always meant the Chinese quarter, a ghetto called "Chinatown." It was in Chinatown that the lonely Chinese laborer could find fellowship, companions, social familiarity, and solace. Chinatown acted as a partial buffer against the prejudices, hatreds, and depredations of hostile whites. Chinatown included the offices and hostelries of the various Chinese benevolent and protective associations, places where one could get a bunk for the night, some food, a stake, and a knowledge of the number, kinds, and conditions of available jobs. Chinatown also housed the Chinese elite—the merchants of the ghetto—who acted as spokesmen for and protectors of the laborers and who held the latter in a state of political dependence and debt bondage. The Chinatowns of America and elsewhere[96] cannot be said to be either the creatures of white racism, on the one hand, or of the congregative sentiments of the Chinese on the other. Rather, they must be seen as a complex emergent produced by these two elements acting simultaneously. A powerful sense of group feeling and many social needs found institutionalized expression in Chinatown at the same time that white aversion and hostility gave added reasons for those Chinese institutions to continue to flourish.

Chinese Social Organization

The Chinese quarters of San Francisco and the other cities where Chinatowns have been established are characterized by a high degree and a complex mesh of organization. To the present day, most Americans are unaware of the actual nature and functions of Chinese associations and tend to regard them in unilluminating stereotypy. There are three basic types of association established in Chinatown, and in addition there are subsidiary and ancillary groupings, and, at the apex of the organizational pyramid, a confederation of associations which tends to govern the community. First there are clans. Clans have their origin in the Chinese lineage communities so prevalent in southeastern China, communities which united their male inhabitants with bonds of blood loyalty based on descent from a common ancestor.[97] Overseas, the lineage unit was replaced by a net sprung wider than the original geographically-compact village of origin to include all those bearing the same surname. The clan provided the boundaries of the incest taboo by prohibiting marriage within the same surname group.[98] Clan officials established hostelries for their kinsmen, and the clan association became a kind of immigrant aid society providing food, shelter, employment, protection, and advice. The clan further served to remind the sojourner of his ties to village and family in China, and, in the absence of the original lineal authorities, it assumed a role *in loco parentis.*[99] In some instances, clans obtained monopolies over some trades or professions in Chinatown and effectively resisted encroachments on these monopolies by ambitious Chinese from other clans.[100] More recently, clan authority has been undermined by the acculturation of Chinese born in America and by a resentment against both its traditional despotism and the clans' failure to ameliorate social conditions.[101]

In addition to clans, however, there developed among overseas Chinese a functionally similar but structurally different type of association. The *hui kuan* united all those who spoke a common dialect, hailed from the same district of origin in China, or belonged to the same tribal or ethnic group. The *hui kuan,* like the clan, originated in China, and by the mid-nineteenth century there were associations of this type throughout the Celestial Empire. In many ways, these Chinese associations were similar to those immigrant aid and benevolent societies formed by Europeans in America, and the German term which has been applied to the latter, *Landsmannschaften,* is applicable to the Chinese *hui kuan* as well.[102]

The several *Landsmannschaften* established in San Francisco and other cities where Chinese dwelt served as caravansaries, hostelries, credit associations, and employment agencies to their members. They also represented their constituencies in dealings with the other *Landsmannschaften* and with white officials. Finally, they conducted arbitration and mediation hearings between individuals and groups and adjudicated disputes. In San Francisco, Vancouver, and New York City, the several *hui kuan* confederated together with other associations—including, often, clans and secret societies—to form a supra-community association. The Chinese Benevolent Association, as it is usually called, provides for Chinatown-wide governance on the one hand and for a united front in relations with white America on the other.[103] During the first half-century of Chinese settlement in America, the consolidated association of *hui kuan* commanded at the least the grudging allegiance and obedience of the toiling Chinese laborers and the respect of many well-meaning whites; however, in more recent times the association's alleged involvement in illegal immigration, its failure to meet the needs of San Francisco's new Chinese immigrant youth, its conservative and traditional orientation toward welfare, and its anachronistic appearance to acculturated American-born Chinese have led to a certain decline in its community power and a slight dampening of its popularity with white America.[104] Nevertheless, it retains considerable authority and can still exert sanctions against recalcitrant and defalcating Chinese in the ghetto.[105]

The third major type of organization in Chinatown is the secret society. Like the clan and the *hui kuan*, the secret society originated in China, where for centuries it had served as the principal agency for protest, rebellion, and banditry. It also provided a haven for those who blamed officialdom for their agricultural or professional failures, those who had been expelled from their villages, expunged from their lineages, or who had run afoul of the law.[106] After 1644, in Kwangtung and Fukien, secret societies were the most notorious opponents of Manchu rule, and for more than 250 years they kept up a sporadic guerrilla war against Ch'ing officials, seaport towns, and wealthy merchants. The overseas branches contributed to Sun Yat-sen's revolution in 1911, but in China secret societies continued to plague both revolutionary forces and republican power holders—both of which tried to crush or co-opt them—well into the middle of the twentieth century. After the advent of the Communist regime, attempts were again made to "coordinate" them or stamp them out, although it is by no means clear how successful these efforts have been.[107]

The migrants from Kwangtung and Fukien in the nineteenth century included not a few of the members of the Triad Society, the most famous of China's clandestine associations. In nearly every overseas Chinese community of size, secret societies sprang up as chapters of this society, or as models based upon it. In Malaya, an area in which much information on these societies has been gathered, the several secret fraternal brotherhoods not only organized much of the social, economic, political, criminal, and recreational life of the Chinese Community, but also played a significant role in the industrial and political development and the foreign relations of the British colony.[108]

In the United States and Canada, Chinese secret societies were established by the early immigrants in the cities and also in the outlying areas, where Chinese miners gathered together to organize the meager elements of livelihood and daily life. In the mining country of British Columbia, for example, a Chinese secret society provided a carefully-run hostelry, adjudicated disputes, and regulated the boundaries of the claims.[109] In the cities, the secret societies soon took over control of gambling and prostitution in the American Chinatowns, and it is with these activities rather than with their political or eleemosynary work that they are most often associated in the minds of non-Chinese in America. The different associations often fell out with one another; their so-called "tong wars"—in actual fact, violent altercations which involved clans, *hui kuan,* and secret societies—are a frequent source of apocryphal history and stereotypy of the Chinese in America. The charitable works of secret societies were confined for the most part to mutual aid to their own constituents, the establishment of buildings and clubhouses where fraternity might be found, and, in recent years, some care and solicitation for their aged and infirm members. Political activities of the secret societies in North America were limited to occasional interest in the fortunes of China's regimes, and they did not interfere or participate in the national politics of the United States or Canada. At the turn of the century and in the decade thereafter, Sun Yat-sen obtained considerable financial support from chapters of the *Chih-kung T'ang* in North America.[110] In San Francisco, over two million dollars in revolutionary currency were printed, while in rural California a few hundred inspired Chinese young men drilled in preparation to join the fighting forces of Sun's revolution.[111] When Dr. Sun was stranded without funds in New York City at a crucial moment in the revolution, Seto May-tong, a Triad Society official who was to continue to exercise influence on the international relations of China and secret societies for more than thirty years, raised the necessary funds to finance his fateful return to China. In 1912, Seto mortgaged the society's buildings in Victoria, Vancouver, and Toronto, raising $150,000 for the revolution.[112]

In more recent years Chinese secret societies may have lost

some of their erstwhile functions and declined in influence and power. Their unity in support of Sun Yat-sen collapsed with the failure of the Republic to establish consensus and legitimacy. Although the Triad Society reorganized as a political party in 1947, it was ineffectual in arranging a peace between the Communist and Kuomintang forces, and has since been devoid of political influence.[113] Meanwhile, in the Chinatowns of America, prostitution and gambling—the traditional sources of secret society revenue—have declined with the infirmity and death of the bachelor immigrants, the establishment of families in America, and the acculturation of the American-born Chinese.[114] Finally, the general rejection of traditional Chinese societies by the present generation of immigrants and Chinese-Americans has added to secret society desuetude.[115] At the present time it would appear that, barring some unforeseen source for their rejuvenation, Chinese secret societies will soon disappear from the American scene.

The Shortage of Women

The principal social problem affecting the Chinese in America was the shortage of women amongst them. So few Chinese women came to America that it was not until the middle of the twentieth century that there occurred even a proximity in the balancing of the sex ratio. During the entire period of unrestricted immigration (1850–1882), a total of only 8,848 Chinese women journeyed to American shores. In that same period, over 100,000 men had arrived in the United States. Many of the women could not stand the rigors of life in America and died or returned to China. By 1890, only 3,868 Chinese women were reported to be in the country. The number of Chinese males continued to grow during the latter three decades of the nineteenth century. In 1860, the census reported 33,149 male Chinese; in 1870, 58,633; in 1880, 100,686; and in 1890 there were 102,620 Chinese men in America. Only in 1900 did the census of Chinese males reveal a halt in the growth of this portion of the Chinese population in America. In that year, 85,341 Chinese males were reported. Between 1860 and 1890, the ratio of Chinese males per one hundred Chinese females was alarmingly high: 1,858 in 1860; 1,284 in 1870; 2,106 in 1880; 2,678 in 1890; and 1,887 in 1900.[116]

The imbalance in the sex ratio was slowly reduced during the first half of the twentieth century. By 1920, despite the birth of a few females among the Chinese in America, the males still far outnumbered the females: for every one hundred women there were more than 695 men. By 1960, the situation had been only partially mitigated. The number of males had grown to 135,430, but the number of females was only 100,654.[117] The low number of females among the Chinese in America, and elsewhere,[118] has been one of the most salient features shaping their personal, social and community life.[119]

Chinese custom held that, ideally, a wife should remain in the household of her husband's parents even in the event that her husband went abroad. Should his parents die in his absence, the wife was expected to perform the burial and mourning rites.[120] Village headmen often secured a prospective emigrant's loyalty to his village by requiring that he marry before his departure and that he promise to remit money for the support of his wife, family, and the village community.[121] Overseas, the clan or *hui kuan* often assumed the obligation of collecting the remittances from the laboring immigrants and sending them to the appropriate villages in China.[122] The lonely laborer toiled in the hope that one day he would return to his wife and family as a wealthy and respected man. In fact, this rarely occurred; instead the sojourner was usually forced to put off his remigration to China year after year. The promise of America's gold turned to dross, but he labored still. For some there was a temporary respite in a visit to China, the siring of a son there, and the hope, sometimes realized, that the son would join the father in the American adventure when he came of age.[123]

If Chinese custom, which was often misunderstood in America,[124] prevented Chinese women from joining their husbands overseas in the first three decades of unrestricted immigration, American law continued the bar against them after 1882. Ac-

cording to the Chinese Exclusion Act of that year, as inter-
preted by the courts two years later,[125] a Chinese woman acquired the legal status of her husband upon marriage. Thus, the
wives of Chinese laborers were excluded in the same law which
excluded Chinese laborers from coming to the United States. In
the many changes made in the immigration laws before they were
all repealed and a quota system imposed in 1943, the few liber-
alizations that were granted were applied almost exclusively to the
Chinese wives of American citizens and the wives and offspring
of Chinese merchants and other classes exempted in the original
exclusion act.[126]

The consequences of the barring of Chinese women were
many and tragic. In the rural mining areas, the few Chinese
women who had come abroad often became unwilling prostitutes
servicing the sexual needs of homeless, lonely Chinese laborers.[127]
"The Chinese are hardly used here," wrote Horace Greeley from
a California mining camp in 1859. He went on to say that "he has
no family here (the few Chinese women brought to this country
being utterly shameless and abandoned), so that he forms no
domestic ties, and enjoys no social standing."[128] "Very few bring
wives with them," wrote Henry K. Sienkiwicz in 1880, in one of
his letters from America, "and for that reason it so happens that
when among ten Chinese occupying a dwelling place there is but
one woman, they all live together with her. I encountered such
examples of polyandry quite frequently, particularly in the
country."[129]

In the cities in which the Chinese congregated, prostitution
was an organized affair under the direct or tributary control of the
secret societies. Young girls were brought to America from China
after they had been kidnapped, sold into indentured servitude by
their parents, captured by pirates or raiding bands, or lured
abroad by a meretricious promise of proxy marriage. Once having arrived in America, they were placed under contract to individual Chinese, or, more often, to brothels in the Chinese quarter.
They might be sold and resold again and again. The brothel
keepers guarded their interest in their "slave girls" by bribing

court interpreters and offering perjured testimony in numerous litigations, and by invoking the assistance of secret society thugs to put off Chinese men who wished to marry a girl under contract.[130]

Organized prostitution and secret society vice domination continued well into the twentieth century.[131] A close observer of Chicago's Chinatown wrote in 1934:

> Women are another temptation. Be it remembered that out of a total of some 5,000 Chinese in Chicago there are only about forty women, and one can imagine the social problem involved. The Chinese Exclusion Act has prevented the Chinese from importing their women. Taking advantage of this situation, the tong men smuggle young girls from China for this purpose. The owner of the prostitution house owns the victims and pays tax to the tong which delivered the girls, and gives to the owner protection. Prostitution houses in the town are in the guise of hotels, and gambling houses, as stores.[132]

Rather than recognizing the source of the problem in America's restrictive immigration laws, most journalists and politicians were content to rail against the Chinese as an immoral people. Only Jacob A. Riis, himself an immigrant, having toured New York's Chinatown in 1890, seemed to grasp the enormity of the problem. He offered a solution: "This is a time for plain speaking on this subject. Rather than banish the Chinaman, I would have the door opened wider—for his wife; make it a condition of his coming or staying that he bring his wife with him. Then, at least, he might not be what he now is and remains, a homeless stranger among us. Upon this hinges the real Chinese question, in our city at all events, as I see it."[133]

The Anti-Chinese Movement in the Cities

The presence of Chinese in large numbers in San Francisco should not have seemed so strange, given the polyglot population already in that city. The heterogeneous denizens of San Francisco were described in an observant report in 1852:

The population of both the State and city was largely increased in 1852. The departures by sea from San Francisco were only 23,196 while there were 66,988 arrivals. This immigration was about double the amount that had taken place in 1851. The immigrants from the Atlantic States generally crossed the Isthmus, while the greater number of European foreigners came around Cape Horn. The Germans, a most valuable and industrious class of men, and the French, perhaps by nature not quite so steady and hard-working a race, though still a useful body of citizens, were year by year arriving in large numbers, and were readily remarked among the motley population. The most untutored eye could distinguish and contrast the natural phlegm and common-sense philosophy of the fat Teuton, and the "lean and hungry look" and restless gestures of the Celt . . . . The English, Scotch and Irish immigrants, were also numerous, but their characteristics, although something different, were less distinguishable from those of native Americans than were the manners and customs of other foreigners. Besides there were always arriving numerous specimens of most other European nations—Spaniards, Portuguese, Italians, Swiss, Greeks, Hungarians, Poles, Russians, Prussians, Dutch, Swedes, Danes, Turks, too—all visited California. Many of them went to the mines, although a considerable proportion never left San Francisco. The country and city were wide enough to hold them all, and rich enough to give them all a moderate independence in the course of a few years . . . .

Upwards of twenty thousand Chinese are included in the general number of arrivals above given. Such people were becoming very numerous in San Francisco . . . at one period of 1852 there were supposed to be about 27,000 Chinese in the state. A considerable number of people of "color" (*par excellence*) also arrived. These were probably afraid to proceed to the mines to labor beside the domineering white races, and therefore they remained to drudge, and to make much money and spend it in San Francisco, like almost every body else. Mexicans from Sonora and other provinces of Mexico, and many Chilians, and a few Peruvians from South America, were likewise continually coming and going between San Francisco and the ports of their own countries. The Chinese immigrants had their mandarins, their merchants, rich, educated, and respectable men, in San Francisco; but all the Mexicans

and Chilians, like the people of negro descent, were only of the
commonest description. The women of all these various races were
nearly all of the vilest character, and openly practiced the most
shameful commerce. The lewdness of fallen white females is shock-
ing enough to witness, but it is far exceeded by the disgusting practices of these tawny visaged creatures.[134]

As late as 1875, San Francisco still attracted comment because of its many peoples, cosmopolitan atmosphere, and colorful character. Samuel Wells Williams, the noted missionary to
China, wrote of it in tones of genuine rapture:

San Francisco is probably the most cosmopolitan city of its
size in the world. Nowhere else are witnessed the fusing of so many
races, the juxtaposition of so many nationalities, the Babel of so
many tongues. Every country on the globe, every state and prin-
cipality, almost every island of the sea, finds here its representative.
Your next door neighbor may be a native of Central Asia; your
vis-a-vis at the restaurant table may have been reared in New Zea-
land; the man who does your washing may have been born under
the shadow of the great wall of China; the man who waits on you at
table may be a lascar from the East Indies. If you go to the theater,
you may find sitting next to you a lady from the Sandwich Islands;
if you go to the Opera, you may hear, in the pauses of the music,
French, German, Italian, Spanish, Russian, Swedish, Modern
Greek, spoken by people dressed in the most scrupulous evening
costume. If you take a ride in the horse-cars, you may find yourself
wedged in between a parson from Massachusetts and a parsee from
Hindostan; if you go to the bank, you may be jostled by a gentle-
man from Damascus, or a prince of the Society Islands. In three
minutes' walk from your place of business, you enter an Oriental
City—surrounded by the symbols of a civilization older than that
of the Pharaohs."[135]

Yet, the strange customs, peculiar habits, and frugal life of
the Chinese seemed to astonish, alarm, or disgust the San Franciscans within a short time after the arrival of Chinese laborers.
Chinese merchants, with their indispensable supply of hot cooked

foods, *objets d'art,* and household necessities, were a small but favored group. Chinese laborers were regarded, on the other hand, as unfair competition in the mines and elsewhere, and as morally degenerate, socially undesirable, and politically irrelevant. The derision of the Chinese, the hatred directed against them, and the vicious half-truths and distortions that were to make up the anti-Chinese stereotype were already visible in 1852. Although, according to San Francisco's annalists of that year, the Chinese were described as "generally quiet and industrious members of society, charitable among themselves, not given to intemperance and the rude vices which drink induces, and . . . reputed to be remarkably attached to their parents," they were despised in California:

> The manners and habits of the Chinese are very repugnant to Americans in California. Of different language, blood, religion, and character, inferior in most mental and bodily qualities, the China-man is looked upon by some as only a little superior to the Negro, and by others as somewhat inferior. It is needless to reason upon such a matter. Those who have mingled with "celestials" have commonly felt before long an uncontrollable sort of loathing against them. "John's" person does not smell very sweetly; his color and the features of his face are unusual; his penuriousness; his lying, knavery, and natural cowardice are proverbial; he dwells apart from white persons, herding only with country-men, unable to communicate his ideas to such as are not of his nation, or to show the better part of his nature. He is poor and mean, somewhat slavish and crouching, and is despised by the whites, who would only laugh in derision if even a divine were to pretend to place the two races on an equality. In short there is a strong feeling,—prejudice it may be, —existing in California against all Chinamen, and they are nick-named, cuffed about and treated very unceremoniously, by every other class.[136]

That the racial hostility toward the Chinese stemmed in great measure from their alleged competition with urban white labor was indicated in 1852, when the California State Senate turned down Senator Tingley's infamous Bill No. 63, "An Act to En-

force Contracts and Obligations to Perform Work and Labor,"
commonly known as the "Coolie Bill."[137] In the committee's
minority report, eventually adopted by the Senate, Senator Philip
Roach, who was to be a leader in the fight for Chinese exclusion
for the next thirty years, wrote that he did not oppose the importation of Oriental contract labor for agriculture: "There is ample
room for its employment in draining the swamplands, in cultivating rice, raising silk, or planting tea. Our State is supposed to
have great natural advantages for those objects; but if these
present not field enough for their labor, then sugar, cotton, and
tobacco invite their attention. For these special objects I have no
objection to the introduction of contract laborers, provided they
are excluded from citizenship; for those staples cannot be culti-
vated without 'cheap labor'; but from all other branches I would
recommend its exclusion." Roach's conclusion about Chinese in
the skilled labor occupations was quite emphatic. "I do not want
to see Chinese or Kanaka carpenters, masons, or blacksmiths,
brought here in swarms under contracts, to compete with our
own mechanics, whose labor is as honorable and as well entitled
to social and political rights as the pursuits designated 'learned
professions.' "[138] By the 1870's, California labor's "social and
political rights" took for form of an organized movement ded-
icated to the restriction of Chinese immigration and the exclusion of Chinese workers from the labor market.

After two decades of mining and railroad building, work
which had kept large numbers of Chinese away from the cities, the
Chinese began to settle down in the urban Chinatowns of the West
and to become a principal part of the labor force in newly-de-
veloping urban industries. During the 1870's and 1880's, Chinese
in San Francisco were employed in woolen, textile, clothing, shoe,
cigar, and gunpowder manufacturing, and in a few other industries which at that time played a vital part in the city's economy.[139]
When the depression of the 1870's put large numbers of white
laborers out of work, the Chinese workers became the objects of
labor union hostility. Popular demagogues—of whom Denis Kearney was the most famous[140]—railed against their presence in

industries, which, they held, rightly belonged to white labor exclusively. Mob actions against the Chinese were organized, harassing laws were passed, and eventually the Chinese were driven out of the industries and in many cases out of the cities as well.

The polemics against the Chinese were inflammatory and exaggerated allegations against their character and culture, and they served as incitements to riot and abuse. Mark Twain, one of the most acute observers of the Western scene, bitterly satirized the mistreatment of Chinese, calling attention to the unequal protection of the laws, the popular prejudices, and the injurious practices from which they suffered daily. He had hoped that the Burlingame Treaty of 1868 would put an end to these abuses, but when its protective provisions were winked at, he fulminated against the street boys and politicans, workers and legislators who perpetrated torture and terror on the inoffensive Chinese. As he so carefully observed, the popular attacks on the Chinese were not simply the outrages of sick or savage individuals, but rather they were the product of a campaign of Sinophobic vilification which had been created by the political, labor, and media leaders.[141] Similarly, Thomas Nast, the political cartoonist, turned his sharp pen to satirizing the inconsistent laws and hate-ridden ideologies which barred Chinese from citizenship and the franchise and which condemned them to be the mud-sills of America. Later, however, Nast appears to have withdrawn the bite from his criticism and to have accepted the permanent place of Chinese in this country as an abused minority.[142] Negro leaders such as Frederick Douglass carefully distinguished their opposition to the coolie trade and to the exploitation of Chinese laborers from any opposition to Chinese as laborers or citizens,[143] but occasionally a California Negro journalist would take up the anti-Chinese cry, contrasting the latter's alleged inability to assimilate with the rapidly Americanizing Negro.[144] As the racist movement spread throughout the United States, the anti-Chinese diatribes became confused with those levelled against the Negro. Comparisons, sometimes favoring one, sometimes the other, were made, but in the end both Negro and Chinese were declared inimical and inferior to white society in general and to white labor in particular.[145]

The demagogic voice of Denis Kearney of California was a major factor in elevating the anti-Chinese movement to national importance. In a letter to Lord Bryce, Kearney defended himself against Bryce's criticism, stating, "My only crime seems to have been that I opposed the Mongolization of my State in the interest of our own people and their civilization."[146] The Workingmen's Party of California, led by Kearney, adopted the slogan "The Chinese Must Go," and, as its numbers and influence increased, it affected California politics and legislation in a remarkable manner. In 1879, it sent a large and vociferous delegation to the state's Constitutional Convention and played an important part in bringing about the infamous Article XIX of the California Constitution. In its vitriolic volley against the Chinese, the Workingmen's Party rose to new heights of rhetorical invective:

> The Chinese coolie represents the most debased order of humanity known to the civilized world. No touch of refinement can ever reach him. He comes to this country in a condition of voluntary servitude, from which by the insidious precautions of the Chinese Six Companies, under whose auspices this immigration is carried on, he is scarcely ever able to escape—brings with him all the loathsome and vicious habits of his native country.
>
> No amount of association or example can change in the least iota his repulsive filthiness, or wean him in the slightest degree from the ways of his race. His personal habits are of the most loathsome. He knows nothing of the family relation, nothing of the sanctity of an oath, regards no right of property except as controlled through absolute fear, and utterly refuses to assimilate in any measure with the people to whom his presence is a curse. As a race, the thirty years of their presence in California has not been able to influence them to a solitary change of habit. They maintain their separate dress, retain their language and religion, institute their own secret courts, levying fines and enforcing decrees, even to the applying of the death sentence, in utter defiance of the laws of the State.
>
> They establish and carry on the most thorough and complete system of gambling, protect and encourage debauchery in its worst

form, and under the cover of their laws, openly provide the most polluted system of prostitution ever known. Wherever they locate as a class in a city or town, it is as if the horrid touch of leprosy had grasped it. Straightway all Caucasian civilization is driven away from the quarter they settle upon; property values are destroyed, and as is the case in San Francisco a proscribed quarter known as "Chinatown" is made, with as exactly defined limits and as complete an isolation from the civilized portion of the community as the line by the Great Wall which divided their own country from Tartary.

Disgusting and nauseating as is the contemplation of the personal habits of the race, it is, however, to the influence which their competition with the intelligent and civilized labor of the State in all our industries will have upon the future, that the people are looking with most concern, and from which unwholesome and unnatural competition the people are anxiously seeking for relief . . . .[147]

The vicious anti-Chinese stereotype was perhaps never so well combined with a fanatical religious anthropology and the racist interests of white labor organizations as in the testimony presented by Frank M. Pixley before the Senate committee investigating Chinese immigration in 1877:

The Chinese are inferior to any race God ever made . . . . I think there are none so low . . . . Their people have got the perfection of crimes of 4,000 years . . . . The Divine Wisdom has said that He would divide this country and the world as a heritage of five great families; that to the Blacks He would give Africa; and Asia he would give to the Yellow races. He inspired us with the determination, not only to have prepared our own inheritance, but to have stolen from the Red Man, America; and it is now settled that the Saxon, American or European groups of families, the White Race, is to have the inheritance of Europe and America and that the Yellow races are to be confined to what the Almighty originally gave them; and as they are not a favored people, they are not to be permitted to steal from us what we have robbed the American savage of . . . . I believe the Chinese have no souls to save, and if they have, they are not worth the saving . . . .

The burden of our accusations against them is that they come in conflict with our labor interests; that they can never assimilate with us; that they are a perpetual unchanging and unchangeable alien element that can never become homogeneous; that their civilization is demoralizing and degrading to our people; that they degrade and dishonor labor; that they never become citizens, and that an alien, degraded labor class, without desire of citizenship, without education and without interest in the country it inhabits, is an element both demoralizing and dangerous to the community within which it exists.[148]

Sparked by the agitation of labor leaders and politicians, the urban anti-Chinese movement entered a violent phase. Riots against the Chinese occurred in the major cities of the West. The first significant urban uprising took place in San Francisco in 1869,[149] and another far more serious riot occurred in the midst of a tong war in Los Angeles' Chinatown on October 24, 1871. After two policemen and a bystander had been killed, a white mob descended on the Chinese quarter and in four hours killed at least nineteen Chinese, including women and children, burned several buildings, and looted the shops.[150] Six years later, unemployed laborers burned and looted San Francisco's Chinese ghetto for several weeks without any significant interference by the public agencies of law enforcement.[151] In 1880, an anti-Chinese riot occurred in Denver.[152] Five years later, uprisings against the Chinese occurred in Rock Springs, Wyoming, and in Tacoma and Seattle, Washington.[153] In 1907, labor-inspired agitation caused a mob of 15,000 white persons, led by some of the city's most prominent citizens, to descend on the Chinese and Japanese quarters of Vancouver, British Columbia; in response, the Orientals called a city-wide general strike which was only settled after intervention by the King of England and his representative, William Lyon Mackenzie King.[154] Riots and assaults on the Chinese also occurred in smaller cities and towns of the West: in Gold Hill and Virginia City, Nevada, in 1869; in Martinez, California, in 1871; in Truckee, California, in 1878, a riot during which a thousand Chinese were driven out; and in many other towns from Napa to Eureka in California, and elsewhere.[155]

Anti-Chinese legislation was of three kinds. The first consisted of state and ultimately of federal laws to restrict the immigration of Chinese or to exclude them altogether from this country. California experimented for twenty-five years with immigration laws which were consistently declared unconstitutional. Only after the anti-Chinese movement had escalated from a sectional to a national issue did the federal government pass the first exclusion act. A second type of law sought to eliminate Chinese from those occupations in which they allegedly competed "unfairly" with white labor. Finally, a number of laws were passed which had either a punitive or harassing intent.

Among the laws passed in California, perhaps the most infamous was Article XIX of the State Constitution, added in the Convention of 1879. This amendment forbade the employment of Chinese in any corporation formed in the state, and on any state, municipal, and county public works, and provided for legislation whereby any city or town might expel its Chinese inhabitants. Much of this amendment was rendered inoperative by judicial decisions.[156] Additional city and state ordinances adversely affected Chinese laundrymen, fishermen, and farmers. San Francisco sought to limit the activities of Chinese washmen by laws which limited the hours, arbitrarily licensed the laundry buildings, and taxed persons who used poles to deliver goods, or who traveled from house to house without a vehicle or horse. Some of these laws survived judicial scrutiny, but most of them fell before the unusually sharp eyes of the justices of the Supreme Court.[157] In other states, including Nevada and Montana,[158] laws or collective action sought the elimination of the peaceful Chinese laundrymen. Chinese fishermen were excluded from fishing by a law excluding aliens ineligible for citizenship from obtaining a license. After this ordinance ran afoul of the courts, a tax law made fishing expensive. California's second law denying fishing licenses to aliens ineligible for citizenship was passed after Chinese became eligible for naturalization and was directed against the Japanese. It, too, was declared unconstitutional.[159] Under the guise of protecting land and resources from aliens, California forbade non-naturalizable aliens from obtaining land in 1913, and only after four decades of fruitless legal challenges was this anti-Oriental legislation declared void.[160] Even though much of California's anti-Chinese legislation was declared unconstitutional, its intent was realized by successful labor agitation which resulted in the firing of Chinese workers in nearly every urban industry in which they had thrived, and their retreat into Chinatown.[161]

The most outrageous of the punitive and harassing legislation were the "lodging house" and "queue-cutting" ordinances passed in San Francisco and subsequently enacted as state laws. A law requiring five hundred cubic feet of air space for each person inhabiting any public hostelry was enforced solely against the Chinese after 1873, and when the Chinese combined to resist the law by refusing to pay the fines and crowding the jails so that there was less than five hundred cubic feet of air space per person in them, the Board of Supervisors retaliated with a vengeance. A vehicle tax on Chinese laundrymen, a prohibition on returning the dead to China, and a public health ordinance ordering the cutting of queues were proposed and sent on to the mayor for signature. Mayor Alvord vetoed the ordinances, but in 1876 they were enacted over the signature of Mayor Bryant. A court case against these laws was begun, and on July 7, 1879, the Circuit Court of the United States invalidated the law that had forced Chinese to be deprived of the badge of citizenship of the Chinese empire. The prohibition on the removal of the dead from county burial plots, unless a physician's certificate was obtained, was upheld by the Supreme Court in the same year.[162]

In addition to abuse by outraged mobs, victimization and deprivation by legislative enactments, and discriminatory attacks by organized labor, the Chinese were also denied the right to testify in California courts and were segregated in several of the states' public schools. According to a ruling by California's twenty-nine year old Chief Justice, Chinese were declared to be Indians and thus ineligible to testify in any case involving a white man. This ruling, making Chinese vulnerable to any kind of otherwise illegal treatment by whites so long as only Chinese witnessed the evil, remained in force from 1854 to 1875.[163] California's Superintendent of Education complained bitterly of the presence of Chinese and other minorities in the public schools in 1859: "Had it been intended by the framers of the education law that the children of the inferior races should be educated side by side with the whites, it is manifest the census would have included children of all colors. If this attempt to force Africans, Chinese, and Diggers into one school is persisted in it must result in the ruin of the schools. The great mass of our citizens will not associate on terms of equality with these inferior races; nor will they consent that their children should do so."[164] The state legislature acquiesced to Superintendent Moulder's request, and in 1860 delegated to him the power to withhold public funds from any school which admitted the proscribed minorities. Provision for separate schools was made, and a Chinese school operated irregularly in San Francisco after 1860. In later years, modifications of the law permitted the admission of non-whites if whites did not object, but this law of 1866 had little effect in subsequent years. Chinese brought suit to desegregate the state's public schools in 1902 but were unsuccessful.[165] Twenty-three years later, Chinese in Mississippi failed in another attempt to desegregate schools and subsequently refused to send their children to the schools established for "colored" pupils.[166] Since 1954, school segregation has been illegal, but *de facto* segregation still persists in the Chinese as well as other non-white ghettos.

Conclusion

The Chinese were truly strangers in a strange land. They had come suddenly to a frontier area, bringing with them cherished values and deeply ingrained customs which, together with their physical distinctiveness, caused them to stand out and apart from the general population. It would not be unfair to point out that the Chinese had very few friends or sympathizers in the American West. Neither radicals nor reactionaries, liberals or conservatives, were interested in defending—much less understanding—them. The radical intellectuals and labor leaders were, with rare exceptions, notorious for their fulminations against the hapless Chinese.[167] Reactionaries, racists, demagogues, nativists, and know-nothings seized upon "the Chinese question" to ride to power in California. Occasionally Protestant missionaries, men such as A. W. Loomis and Otis Gibson, took a sympathetic interest in and assumed a protective posture toward the Chinese. But when conversions proved to be few in number, these brave souls deserted the field and in some instances turned against their former charges. The Catholics remained almost universally opposed to the Chinese, preferring to serve their Irish flock and even to minister to its Sinophobia.[168] A few officials and attorneys, possessed of a sense of *noblesse oblige* or moved to defend civil rights—among them Hall McAllister, Colonel Frederick A. Bee, and Benjamin S. Brooks—accepted the challenge of the Chinese presence and strove manfully to maintain their liberties and defend their lives and property. But these men were only effective in the courts; they could not stop the violence of aroused mobs nor could they counter the invective and organization of the anti-Chinese unions. In the end, the Chinese were forced to retreat behind the "walls" which prejudice and discrimination had erected —they returned to the ghetto and inside it attempted to build a secure if not prosperous life.

By the turn of the century, the Chinese were isolated, neglected, and demoralized. Located inside the Chinatowns of American cities, they achieved some sense of cultural freedom, a relaxation of tensions, and a precarious independence. Some found a new sense of freedom in giving support to Sun Yat-sen's liberation movement for China; a few prospered as merchants and gained political and social power in the ghettos; but most remained homeless and trapped, too poor to return to China, and too oppressed to enter fully into American society. Sojourners without wives, they could not produce a second generation which, had it been born, might have succeeded like the second generation of other immigrant groups. Only after 1930 were there enough Chinese women present in America to guarantee that a new generation of significant proportions would develop in the following two decades. The much-vaunted Chinese family remained but an idea in Chinatown for eight remorseless decades.

Today, America and its Chinese are beginning to sense the legacy of the nineteenth century. The children of the immigrants, born in America, growing up in a period of relative tolerance and burgeoning civil rights, educated in public schools and emancipated from Chinese tradition, have left Chinatown for the professions, the suburbs, and the rest of the American dream. To be sure, they still encounter discrimination in housing and in certain occupations, and they must still silently wince at the gauche pretensions of toleration which often accompany white "acceptance."

Meanwhile, inside Chinatown, the old elites, composed of executives of the clans, *hui kuans,* and secret societies, continue to hold sway at the expense of their subjects, over whom they exercise a benevolent but despotic authority. The mass of present-day Chinatowners may be divided into four groups for whom life holds out varying degrees of promise and poverty. The aged bachelors live in tiny, cold, unkempt rooms, suffer from tuberculosis and other diseases not prevalent in the metropolis, and contribute to Chinatown's alarming suicide rate. The shopkeepers and restauranteurs thrive on a tourist trade, but privately worry about the effects of America's foreign policy on their fortunes. The new immigrants find themselves doubly estranged and alienated—they cannot bow to the authority of the Chinatown elites, but they lack the language and skill with which to enter the American mainstream. Some work in the garment sweatshops, eking out a meager living from a production system that was once the horror of every humane Occidental and has now all but disappeared except in Chinatown. The youthful immigrants are angry and militant, and, in their outcry against a seemingly pitiless system, they sound a call like that of Negro and other minorities seeking independence and identity. The American-born school dropouts, those who for one reason or another have not made it into white America, are estranged from their immigrant peers by culture and language, but are enjoined from white or Chinese-American middle-class life by their academic and occupational failures. Imbued with a new spirit born of desperation and vague radicalism, they too have of late assumed the posture of an independent group seeking not assimilation but liberty. Chinatown's future lies with its people. It is as problematic and unpredictable as is America as a whole. One step in understanding its present is a knowledge of its past.

Chapter V

Japanese-Americans: Some Costs of Group Achievement

John Modell

The experience of the Japanese is one of the paradoxes of California history. By almost any social and economic measurement, they are the most successful of the state's minority groups. In recent years, they have suffered little overt discrimination, at least in comparison with other non-white citizens. Yet the "yellow peril" fear of the early twentieth century resulted in one of the most vocal campaigns of racism and prejudice in California history, and no other racial group in the state has experienced mass, systematic removal on the scale of the Japanese relocation of World War II.

In this chapter, Dr. John Modell explores some of the paradoxes of the Japanese experience in California. Dr. Modell is a member of the History Department at the University of Minnesota, specializing in American urban history, immigration, and race relations. Until 1969, he was Director of Research for the Japanese American Research Project at the University of California, Los Angeles. Dr. Modell's articles on the history of the Japanese in California have appeared in recent issues of the *Pacific Historical Review*.

Japanese-Americans: Some Costs of Group Achievement

Carey McWilliams, California's most articulate racial liberal, examined the history of the state's Japanese minority before World War II in terms of the peculiar pattern of race relations the state had long demonstrated: "the cleverly manipulated exploitation . . . of a series of suppressed minority groups which were imported to work in the fields."[1] McWilliams' theme, one common to numerous writers, was that the troubles the Japanese had with Anglo California were typical of the economically profitable bigotry the ruling elite had shown toward successive waves of racially distinguishable migrants. And in part, the schema is applicable, for the history of the Japanese in California, like that of the Indians, Chinese, Mexicans, and Negroes, was "complicated by genuine race feeling," as Theodore Roosevelt began to recognize in the early days of the "Japanese problem."[2] But certain qualities of Japanese–white relations in California have been unique, and help to explain the shift from enmity toward the Japanese-Americans, extending through their expulsion from California and incarceration during World War II, to an appreciation for their racial "success story" since the war.

The Japanese-American story has differed from that of other non-white minorities in two crucial respects: why the whites said they disliked the Japanese minority, and how the Japanese reacted toward the discrimination they, like their colored predecessors and successors, suffered at the hands of the majority.

In 1916, Lincoln Steffens, the perceptive crusading journalist, elicited from Governor Hiram Johnson—no friend to the Japanese—a clear explication of the unique and rather perverse white-Californian attitude toward the Japanese: "Their superiority, their aesthetic efficiency, and their maturer mentality make them effective in competition with us, and unpopular and a menace."[3] The California Japanese were (as we shall see) undeniably able competitors in the economic realm, and as well organized and articulate as they were industrious. The stereotype of the indolent Mexican or the heathen Chinee just did not ring true enough, even to the ears of white Californians, when applied to the Japanese. Rather, wild exaggerations were bandied about his fecundity, his continued allegiance to a threatening foreign power, his economic rapacity, and his "refusal" to become, in the terms of the day, "Americanized."

Two related aspects of the Japanese reaction to such attacks have played an important part throughout the eighty-odd years of the history of the group in California. The first aspect is the near unanimity with which the group made their public response. A clearly designated set of spokesmen answered for the entire body of their fellows, spokesmen notable in the Japanese community as leaders of ethnic organizations, religious persons, newspapermen, and businessmen. And, second, their response was always a measured one, for theirs was a strategy of racial accommodation. Faced with the need to interpret a hostility they did not believe was just, and to see in their present situation some hope for betterment so that their children might know a more friendly setting than they had, the immigrants subscribed substantially to the determinedly patient themes enunciated by their spokesmen. Though the Japanese were hurt inwardly by the disdain shown them, they would not show it. Rationality rather than recrimination was the theme of their reply to the whites; self-assertion would be temporarily deferred while an economic beachhead was established.

One further contrast between the Japanese-Americans and other California minorities must not be overlooked: the role of the mother country. For Japan was not only one continent closer to California than it was to the District of Columbia, it was also competent, proud, assertive, and—most important—increasingly powerful. When the federal government "evacuated" over one hundred thousand Japanese-American aliens and citizens to inland "relocation" centers during World War II, the avowed reason was the plausible military threat presented by Japan, and the possible connivance in Japanese schemes by some unknown number of local Japanese-Americans. Although the misconception of the loyalty of local Japanese sprang from racial prejudice, the enormity of the blight upon the conscience of Anglo California should not obscure the fact that the power and assertiveness of the Japanese nation had even decades earlier been a component in California's hostile attitude toward its Japanese minority.

Ordinary motivations first brought Japanese migrants to American shores. Overwhelmingly, the newcomers were sons of farmers, "excess" population with no clear economic function in their native land. To them, the newly developing American Pacific Coast—with its insatiable demands for willing workers with strong backs—began to call in the late 1880's. By far the largest number of Japanese migrants came to the United States intending to remain only a few years and to return to Japan with fresh funds to enlarge their family farms. The first year that Japanese migration amounted to so many as one thousand was 1891; the figure exceeded ten thousand for several years in the 1900's and 1910's. In 1930, after the Japanese migration to America was virtually complete, a total of 97,000 Japanese (immigrants and their children) were enumerated in California, or seven in ten Japanese in the continental United States. This concentration, however, constituted only 1.7 per cent of the total population of the Golden State, even though since 1910 the Japanese had been its largest non-white minority. Of the 1930 California Japanese, only a small majority were urban; the one-third who were counted in the rural farm population were a smaller proportion than had been enumerated in 1910, but greatly exceeded that of most American immigrant groups at this time.

When the first Japanese had arrived, they were perceived (when the white residents took notice of them at all) as replacements for the Chinese, whose number had been decreasing since the Chinese Exclusion Act of 1882. The Chinese population in

America remained stable at about one hundred thousand between 1880 and 1890; at the latter date, Japanese residents numbered approximately two thousand. In the following decade, Chinese departures approximately equalled Japanese arrivals, and it was only between 1900 and 1910 that the total number of Orientals increased substantially, as Japanese arrivals outnumbered Chinese departures. The same explicitly racial reasoning that had denied the privilege of naturalization to Chinese was extended to the Japanese, and jobs were offered the new arrivals in the old Chinese lines of gang labor on railroads and farms.

The Japanese immigrant was not a pioneer. Rather, he usually entered where others had uncovered opportunities and he exploited some portion of these with a thoroughness his predecessors had not shown. The Chinese gold miner and railroad builder had preceded most of white society into parts of newly-opened California. Japanese followed the subsequent white influx, and operated in areas and in activities marginal to established white communities. At all times, thus, Japanese in America were engaged with white society in a far more complicated and ambivalent relationship than were the Chinese.

In the first decades of the twentieth century, Japanese had already begun to cut out for themselves a position in the economy of the state that was a source of amazement and discomfort to their white competitors. By this time, to many whites, the "Japanese problem" was already one in which the immigrants had proved themselves too competent: "The Japanese in California must be beaten in such competition by a lowering of the white man's standard of living, or he must be placed in a menial caste and kept there."[4] The hated Chinese was now seen in a somewhat different light by those concerned with the development of California, the *Los Angeles Times,* for example, expressing the wish that the "peaceful, industrious and law-abiding" Japanese would confine their activities somewhat, and "cultivate their gardens, and clean clothes, and make and sell kimonos," like the Chinese.[5]

Characteristic of the Japanese-American economy, and highly vexing to California whites, was a strong drive toward entrepreneurial development. Emboldened to leave their native land by their need for capital for use at home, the Japanese moved briskly toward exploitable sources of money. Long-term wage labor had in this respect a tremendous disadvantage: the limits placed upon it were determined not by the energy or resourcefulness of the employee, but by the will of the employer. Enterprise, on the other hand, however lowly, could usually be made to profit by alertness and self-denial, especially in a young and developing country. This, at any rate, was the Japanese "formula," never explicitly laid out but developed in the first years of Japanese settlement in this country.

Often financed by the products of wage labor and extreme personal frugality, Japanese enterprise tended to start at the fringes of Anglo businesses. Continued self-denial was indispensable in the early stages, as was shrewd choice of line. In the several characteristically "Japanese" businesses, initial growth tended to be followed by an expansion of the types of establishment and often the integration of suppliers with wholesalers and wholesalers with retailers, as well as close mutual self-regulation among competitors within the ethnic group. With the growing Japanese population as a valuable resource, each Japanese industry became interdependent with others, both in strictly economic terms and in terms of interlocking proprietary families and personnel. Rapidly, the Japanese group progressed toward the point where the ethnic group as a whole had many of the characteristics of a purposive economic grouping.

Although somewhat different economic specializations were followed in different parts of the West, the Los Angeles County pattern was typical of the intense and determined Japanese-American search for prosperity. An account of agriculture, the largest Japanese industry there (as in California as a whole) will serve as an example of the pattern of economic growth that propelled the Japanese community into prosperity, on the one hand, and into a symbiotic relationship with whites, oscillating between interdependence and hostility, on the other.

The Japanese entry into Los Angeles agriculture violated, in its daring, the cautions usually appropriate to American farming. Driven by a distinctly speculative desire for large earnings, the Japanese rented small parcels of close-in lands held by white absentees who anticipated future residential subdivision. For such land, the Japanese paid in many instances unusually high rents, and were even more attractive to speculative landlords because they were willing to live temporarily in near-squalor. Close-in lands and meticulous farming methods made it possible for the Japanese to produce superlative fruits and vegetables, a small beginning but one which eventually grew to a near-monopoly of many agricultural products. Following the demands of the market, and displaying a shrewd sense of the crop that would allow the largest return for the smallest amount of capital outlay combined with the greatest amount of labor, they shifted from sugar beets to berries, to lettuce, to celery; of the last, they produced virtually all that was grown in Los Angeles in 1941.

The Los Angeles Japanese were not long content with merely growing produce. At a remarkably early date they entered retailing and wholesaling, completing the vertical integration of the industry (and buttressing this through cooperation and even price-fixing among enterprisers of the Japanese race at each level of the business). The pioneer Japanese in wholesaling were relatively small entrepreneurs, usually men who operated a single stall in the wholesale market rather than holding an interest in a larger concern; they were thus able to give personal attention to the condition of the produce they distributed. Partly through a common sense of Japaneseness and partly through a largely justified belief that Japanese grew the best produce in the county and were most scrupulous in bringing it to market, they dealt most often with growers of their own race. Rather than expanding the scope of their wholesaling enterprises, Japanese entered the fruit-stand business *en masse*. A common Los Angeles ethnic stereotype before World War II was the Japanese vegetable man: polite, a bit peculiar in his English, and able to sell unusually attractive produce.

The development of a distinct if limited prosperity for Japanese in California by means of a minute division of labor along racial lines did not go unnoticed by jealous whites. For the earlier demographically-based anxiety that the yellow race would over-run California was substituted the fear that the Japanese would take over California's agriculture. Initially, the California anti-Japanese movement was urban, and—as had been the Chinese difficulties—based on organized labor. As early as 1904, the California State Federation of Labor had argued that the Japanese were inherently "men of a lower standard of morals, of a lower standard of wages, men of a race that has never assimilated with Caucasians, but which race has always pulled down and pulled down irresistably, the men of the Caucasian race that have been forced into contact with men of the Mongolian race."[6]

In the following year, the labor-dominated government of the city of San Francisco undertook to segregate the insignificant number of Japanese students in the public schools that had earlier been established for the Chinese. Only the intervention of President Theodore Roosevelt (more concerned with Japan's power than with San Francisco's racism) prevented the application of the ordinance. In exchange, Roosevelt extracted from Japan her agreement to limit, voluntarily and without any sign of external compulsion, its issuance of immigrant passports to America to "non-laborers or . . . laborers who, in coming to the continent, seek to resume a formerly acquired domicile, to join a parent, wife or children residing there, or to assume active control of an already possessed interest in a farming enterprise in this country [America]."[7]

Efforts of San Francisco's labor to bring the Japanese menace to the attention of the rest of California were generally unsuccessful at this time, but anti-Japanese agitation had only begun. According to the common notion of the day that California was a "racial frontier" which must be kept safe for white settlement, the arguing point of California's anti-Japanism had shifted by 1913 to stress the threat the Japanese posed to the small farmer.

By this time, awareness of the Japanese had diffused throughout California. While the state legislature debated a bill that would limit the terms on which Japanese could operate farmland in the state, Governor Hiram Johnson received letters indicating the extent to which at least certain vocal elements of his constituency had accepted racial-frontier doctrine. His correspondents could stress economics:

> If you could have seen the white man literally driven out of this valley by the Japanese as I have you would fully appreciate the enormity of this menace .... Six years ago I raised $1650.00 worth of strawberries on one acre in one year .... Soon after that the Japs came in this country and now the berry business is practically all in their hands .... Every Jap displaces at least 3 or 5 white people.

Or they could see things in more geopolitical terms:

> From a *Military* standpoint ..., the logical sequence of Japanese performance is that, of regular systematic preparation for armed invasion and occupancy .... It should be regarded as a fact that a group of Japanese officers *now holding commissions in the Japanese Army* now and for some years past have been resident in Los Angeles and vicinity. That for at least three years past, these officers and their subordinates have been regularly engaged in systematic military *reconnoissance* of Los Angeles and the surrounding country.[8]

But in any case the messages saw an irreconcilable struggle between Japanese and white man, with California farms the immediate prize and the fate of California itself in the balance.

The Alien Land Law of 1913, passed by the California legislature, forbade aliens ineligible to citizenship to purchase farmland in the state or to lease it for more than three years. The law was too loosely drawn, however, to destroy Japanese agriculture or even to reverse its growth. A resumed agitation in 1919 and 1920 was in a sense the most public hearing the "Japanese question" would receive, for California voters were asked to decide at the general election of 1920 upon an amended version of the Alien Land Law. Incumbent United States Senator James D.

Phelan, running at this time for re-election, placed the electorate in the position of guardians of the racial frontier:

> California itself is a monument to its discoverer [Cabrillo, its *white* discoverer]—a State of surpassing beauty and of varied and inexhaustible resources, self-sufficient, complete and unparalleled. Here the civilization of East and West have met for a great trial of strength. One must dominate.[9]

Phelan also stressed the moral turpitude, promiscuous breeding, illegal fishing methods, illegal entry, unsanitary farming practices, unfair competition, and murderous treachery of the California Japanese, and the national ambition and militarism of their fatherland.

The Hearst newspapers, the American Legion, the Native Sons of the Golden West, the California State Grange, and the California State Federation of Labor joined with Phelan in this effort, as did his Republican challenger. California voters responded with a three-to-one margin in favor of abating the Japanese farm menace. But even at this, the apogee of anti-Japanese agitation before World War II, one-quarter of the electorate rejected a point of view that had no important political opposition and little public opposition, except occasionally from the pulpit. No *popularly-based* anti-Japanese organizations were formed at this time that lasted for any appreciable length of time. And despite his furious efforts to gain re-election through his attacks upon the local Japanese, Phelan failed to retain his Senate seat, although it is almost certain that his campaign benefited him by stirring up latent anti-Japanism. White California was racist, undoubtedly; but it was racist in a basically casual way. The racial frontier was accepted as a fact of life. As far as local agitation went, the Immigration Act of 1924, which denied to Japan even a nominal quota of immigrants, merely put a national cachet on this view.

Surely, the Japanese could draw encouragement from these signs, even in their darkest moments. If only the hearts of the decent, unagitated white Californians could be reached, a less hostile accommodation could be achieved. Such a hope—inferring the possibility of rational behavior from the usual indifference of the white public—motivated much of the Japanese-American thinking on how to get along with their neighbors. Of prime importance, of course, was the economic factor: the reason for coming to America in the first place, and the reason that many of the immigrants had stayed beyond the time they had at first intended. Even the attacks of Phelan, even the apparently stringent regulations on Japanese enterprise represented by the two Alien Land Laws, did not prevent the expansion of the Japanese economic structure. In addition, as children came, their stake in America (as well as their legal capacity to get along in it, as native-born citizens) was greater. Many would be going to college, and who knew whether white hostility might not abate in time for them to gain a place as full and equal, as well as prosperous, Americans.

The Japanese first generation, with the cooperation of Japanese consular officials, organized a Japanese Association as early as 1900 to meet white hostility in an organized, orderly fashion. By the 1920's, several broad areas of Japanese-American population had Japanese Associations, whose quasi-official authority coordinated a number of local Japanese Associations, and whose membership in theory embraced the entire Japanese community. Internal disagreements, of course, existed, for any notion of monolithic solidarity in an American ethnic group is ridiculous. But with the important position of the consul to aliens ineligible for citizenship, and with repeated need for legal and political defense against successive agitations, the Japanese Associations had great authority. Even as the strength of the Associations waned in the mid-1920's, the tradition of central determination of group strategy continued, with business and religious associations taking the lead.

The central strategy settled upon was accommodation to the demands—even the patently irrational demands—of the California whites, except in economic matters. The Japanese Association of America, for example, pledged to President Woodrow Wilson in 1919 that they were "advising" their constituents "as best we know how, not to work so hard as to cause their neighbors to criticize them, and to create some leisure for self-development." The Association added that, even so, "it appears . . . rather strange that the Americans should complain of Japanese[-American] industry."[10] The Japanese Associations, and church and lay groups, worked to eliminate Japanese-American crime and to make it unnecessary for Japanese to become dependent upon American charity. Japanese community organizations were very hopeful that their concerted involvement in the white-sponsored "Americanization" movement of the 1910's and 1920's would gain favorable public recognition. At the same time that legislators were working to tighten the Alien Land Law, other state employees, conducting a state-sponsored immigrant-Americanization class, reported as typical their experience with Japanese men, who, "as soon as [they] had learned to read a few words in English, . . . demanded the words of 'America' and were soon putting the words to a rather perverted form of the tune of our national anthem."[11] During World War I, adult California Japanese men bought an average of seventy-five dollars each in war bonds, the Los Angeles Japanese Chamber of Commerce having resolved that "the anti-Japanese feeling among Americans is irrelevant to the bonds."[12] At a point when his constituents were being threatened by sporadic instances of neighborhood anti-Japanese agitation, the President of the Los Angeles Japanese Association told his community that although the fault was basically not within them, nevertheless,

> . . . it must be remembered that if there is anything in our daily conducts [*sic*] which is repugnant to the good customs and manners of America and otherwise objectionable, we must be good enough to change it right away . . . . This is a high time for both the older and younger generation to bring about radical reformation not only in our work and enterprises but also in our thought so that

we may really deserve the respect of the people. It is also to be pointed out that to become stronger and independent socially and financially is to do much with the solution of the anti-Japanese problem.[13]

The emphasis on the two generations in this declaration was typical, even at such an early date as 1923, for a problem that was to gnaw at the Japanese-American community during much of the pre-evacuation period was the disappearance in the American setting of the close familial structure that was so central to social relations in Japan. If the immigrant generation was baffled by its offspring, the offspring were no less confused about how they stood toward their parents; some believed that "the freedom of their children seemed to be a worry to some parents who feared only the worst for their liberty-loving progeny," but such claims oversimplified equally the second generation's love of "liberty" and their parents' fear of it.[14]

Hoping to bridge what they thought was merely a gap in communications, the first generation established Japanese-language schools, which would (after the regular day of public school) emphasize the duties of American citizenship and "teach the Japanese language in order to increase the understanding between parents and children so that they may all enjoy their home life."[15] A great majority of American-born Japanese attended such schools, usually somewhat grimly and with sparse results; even if rudiments of Japanese sentence structure could be taught, the native generation (in the pattern of most American ethnic groups) was not of a mind to learn the glories of Japanese culture. One perceptive first-generation observer later recalled that before the war, American-born Japanese could never easily admit to whites their racial identity without first asserting their nationality: Americans. "All things being equal, if he could convince the American public that despite his physical characteristics and name, he could not speak even a word of Japanese or appreciate Japanese culture, then, he reasoned, they would accept him as an American."[16]

Equally important in making the prewar position of the native-born Japanese-American an uncomfortable one was his unhappy job outlook. First-generation parents had struggled to put their children through high school and college; the youth had performed brilliantly, to the enormous satisfaction of their parents and teachers. But they were quite regularly denied the kinds of jobs to which their education and application ought to have entitled them, and thus were faced with a disillusionment that their parents, without citizenship and for years without illusions about their own chances, had not felt. Hospitals, schools, universities, law firms, and the like did not want Japanese faces, however well trained the minds behind them, and however absent any telltale accent.

The second-generation perspective was dominated by thwarted but thoroughly Americanized goals of personal success, and by an impatience that made their parents' accommodation impossible. First-generation counsel was galling to their children. "Back to the land," for example, was a frequent theme; one leading representative of the first generation urged that "there should be a gradual diminishing of the so-called problem of the lack of vocations for the second-generation people" if only they would "go further by extending into the cattle, cotton, wheat, corn, dairy products industries. Their future is a hopeful one, especially in view of the fact that farmers of other races are abandoning their homes for the cities."[17] To immigrants who had already made this kind of a choice, the problem of the second generation might be "so-called"; but their children wanted to abandon the family farm, along with the caste-like accommodation their parents had accepted for themselves and now were encouraging their children to adopt.

But citizen Japanese-Americans had no better answer to the "white problem" than had the immigrants. A stiff upper lip served temporarily. "The stigma of being a Japanese can only be overcome by surpassing ability," said one young Japanese-American, who professed to appreciate such a pressure as an antidote to the tendency to "mediocrity," of which "the world is full."

Another of his contemporaries decried the promiscuous application of "the time-worn 'emotion-rouser'—racial discrimination" to "every situation which may seem repugnant to an individual of Japanese ancestry. Too often, it is used to excuse oneself for his own shortcomings."[18]

The relocation intervened in a situation that was increasingly unbearable to the maturing second generation. As a denouement, of course, there was nothing comforting about the fact of the relocation. The much-agitated decision to relocate—involving a macabre obeisance throughout every echelon of the federal government to a baseless notion of military necessity—was capped by an avowedly racial interpretation of the war in the Pacific by the military commander at whose word the Japanese were removed.[19]

The several years before the war—as Japan began to appear a threat to America's security—had seen the beginnings of a reawakening of California's traditional hostile interest in its Japanese minority. Even after Pearl Harbor, however, despite some lobbying by newspapers, traditional anti-Japanists, and commercial competitors of the Japanese-Americans, the full hue and cry of California hatred awaited the words and official deeds of men in responsible government positions. The relocation of native-born Japanese was approved by only about one-third of Southern Californians (where newspaper and official comment was particularly rabid and general suspicion at its highest) in mid-February, 1942, two months after Pearl Harbor. But a month and a half later, four in five throughout California supported the policy, by then distinct, of removing both alien and native-born Japanese. The Japanese-Americans, though surprised and shocked, took the blow with a courage that far surpassed stolidity: "It's a great life and a new experience," wrote a twenty-four year-old Japanese-American girl, ten days after relocation. "I am prepared to have fun, no matter what. It's not a grim determination, either . . . . Our being evacuated here [Manzanar, California] in all this beauty at this particular time of year is a sort of rebirth, a beginning of a finer life."[20]

Almost until the end of the war, California had *no* Japanese minority, except for those in two relocation centers. For some white Californians, this was the fulfillment of a long-term ambition; and that Japanese settlement might be permanently dispersed more evenly throughout the country was in fact an avowed policy of many persons of good will, including the leadership of the agency in charge of the relocation centers. But a racially defined policy of internal population transfer began to sound sour to Americans engaged in a war against Hitler, and the racist sentiments of General John L. De Witt, the West Coast military commander, even more so. "Isn't it possible that the seed of discrimination will be sown upon other ethnic groups?" one California organization concerning itself with the return of the evacuees asked when it became clear that Japan was nearly defeated.[21]

Return to California began in early 1945, and soon indicated that the Japanese-Americans had not abandoned the state. By 1950 (as also in 1960), six in ten Japanese-Americans outside of Hawaii were living in California, only a slight decline from the three-quarters recorded in 1940. The returnees were not without friends: officials on all levels of government admitted that they had been mistaken, and the federal government strived to mold public indifference into toleration. The Japanese-Americans had proven their loyalty in battle, after the exigencies of the war and the extraordinary persistence of certain Japanese-Americans in pursuing a policy of cooperation had led to the opening of sections of the armed forces to persons of Japanese extraction. One Californian avowedly hostile to the minority expressed incisively the new state of affairs: "The worst mistake the government made was to let them in the Army. They come back with an arm gone, or a leg gone, and you have to show them consideration."[22]

A by-product of the war was the passing of the first generation as the dominant force in the life of the California Japanese community, partly from aging and partly from the importance of the citizenship of the natives in the controversies and negotiations with wartime authorities. With an end to the virulent anti-Japanism, the Japanese-American community in more ways than ever began to look like any other American ethnic group. One second-generation scholar noted "groups in Los Angeles [that] play golf and take Las Vegas weekends," and that the decline of felt need for the reputation of "goodness" had permitted the third generation to approach "normally" high levels of such indices of disorganization as juvenile delinquency and mental illness.[23]

A more substantial sign of the acceptance of the Japanese-Americans has been in the crucial area of occupational structure. The table below shows that between 1940 and 1960, job patterns

Occupational Distribution of Employed Males in California, 1940-1960: Japanese and Total Population

Occupational type	**1940**		**1950**		**1960**	
	Japanese	*Total*	*Japanese*	*Total*	*Japanese*	*Total*
Professional, technical, and kindred workers	2.7%	8.9%	4.4%	9.8%	15.7%	14.3%
Managers, officials, and proprietors	12.2%	12.4%	8.7%	13.5%	8.2%	12.6%
Clerical and sales workers	9.9%	15.9%	8.9%	15.0%	12.9%	15.5%
Craftsmen, foremen, operatives, and kindred workers	8.1%	33.7%	11.8%	37.6%	20.4%	38.8%
All farm workers	47.1%	12.7%	39.4%	8.9%	31.9%	5.6%
Laborers, service workers, private household workers	20.0%	16.4%	26.8%	15.9%	10.9%	13.2%
	100%	100%	100%	100%	100%	100%
Number of males in labor force:						
Japanese	*30,125*		*24,235*		*44,019*	
Total	*1,841,317*		*2,753,965*		*3,858,815*	

of Japanese males in California gradually approached that of all male Californians. Especially noteworthy is the steady rise of the prestigious category of "professional, technical, and kindred" workers, to a proportion in 1960 *higher* than the statewide average. Part of this, to be sure, was the result of the coming of age of a new and highly-trained generation, but part of the dilemma of this generation before World War II had been that there were not enough positions available even to those with the requisite educations. Conversely, despite a continued Japanese concentration in agriculture, there has been a steady decline in the degree to which the agricultural interest has dominated the community. Greatly reduced, too, by 1960 was the proportion of laborers, household workers, and service workers. Filling the slack have been industrial occupations: craftsmen, foremen, operatives, and kindred workers—positions formerly denied Japanese-Americans on racial grounds.

When the 1970 census shows, at it almost certainly will, that the California Japanese have continued their advance toward the economic success they, like most other immigrant groups before and since, have sought, there will be no outburst of hostility toward them. If anything, their performance will be hailed as a "model," to which earnest whites will urge other groups to conform. The case of the Japanese in California is an indication that white racism is not a simple, irreducible, and unchangeable quantity. Japan played a role in Anglo attitudes toward the Japanese-American minority unmatched by that of the mother country of any other immigrant group. Likewise, the waning of the racial-frontier ideology with the end of World War II has thoroughly altered the intergroup contest California whites so long imagined. The Japanese strategy of radical accommodation, possibly irrational and certainly humiliating in the short run, has in the long run turned out to be a balm to white Californians now worried by men of a different hue.

Chapter VI

White Racism and
Black Response
in California History

Velesta Jenkins

In 1964, California voters overwhelmingly supported Proposition 14, an iniative measure which abolished the state's "fair housing" law. In the same election, the voters also supported overwhelmingly Lyndon Johnson, who had committed himself to strong measures to combat racial segregation. This apparent inconsistency did not surprise veteran observers of California politics, who are accustomed to the contradictory whims of the state's electorate. However, the victory of Proposition 14 did shatter the myth of racial harmony that was supposed to characterize black–white relations in California. And if that myth was shattered by the 1964 election results, it was buried once and for all by the Watts upheaval of 1965.

In fact, however, the state has had a long history of conflict between black and white people, extending back at least as far as the Gold Rush period. In this chapter, Mrs. Velesta Jenkins summarizes a portion of that history. She writes from the perspective of a young black woman who, in her own words, is "an integrationist turned cynic." Mrs. Jenkins is an Instructor in Afro-American History and Black Studies at Laney College in Oakland and a former teacher in the Oakland public schools.

White Racism and
Black Response
in California History

In 1846, the Mexican tolerance that had existed in California was replaced by Anglo-American racism. This racism was practiced against Indians, Mexicans, Orientals, and Afro-Americans.

The slow elimination of slavery in the northern United States after Independence did not mean that Northern racism disappeared. Most Northerners were against slavery, but few encouraged free blacks to come North. Everywhere in the North, free blacks had to exist under Jim Crow laws and were subject to occasional mob violence. Before the Civil War, black people had the vote taken from them in Pennsylvania, New Jersey, and Connecticut.

De Toqueville was shocked to find that racial prejudice was strongest in areas where slavery had never been known. But, since poor whites left the South and sometimes the North to escape the labor competition of black people, it was not strange that the farther west one went, the stronger the segregation became. A slave did not need to be segregated because his mind was already chained, but a free black man in the West was an economic threat, and therefore his activity had to be restricted by (1) denial of the vote, (2) denial of the right to testify, and (3) Jim Crow restrictions on eating places and other social accommodations. In the 1840–1850 period, Oregon and New Mexico passed laws denying public land grants to black people. In Oregon, a black man could not buy real estate of any kind, and some Oregon towns promised a lashing to any black crossing their borders.

[123]

California legislators in the 1850's attempted to pass laws prohibiting the entry of blacks and mulattos into the state. Although these measures were defeated, the state's Constitution of 1849 did prohibit blacks from voting. Antonio Maria Pico, a man with one-eighth black blood, remained silent during the convention proceedings, afraid that mixed bloods, too, would be denied the vote. Many Spanish-speaking blacks and mulattos had been able to hold political office before California became a state, but now Pico was nervous about his nebulous "rights."

Immediately after the American conquest of 1846, the growth of California's black population was slow and usually consisted of slaves accompanying their masters to the West. The first large increase in the black population came after 1850 as a result of the Gold Rush. Several thousand English- and Spanish-speaking blacks participated in the Gold Rush—at least a thousand black people were in California by 1850, and their numbers grew to more than four thousand by 1860. The majority were free men who had come West to make fortunes in business and mining, but some were slaves brought by Southern panhandlers to work the mines, and others were fugitive slaves.

In most mining camps, whites were not allowed to hire Indian or black labor because this was considered unfair competition. To get around this restriction, Southerners formed isolated camps, away from other miners, or pretended that the slaves owned their own mines. Local and state agencies did not enforce the state's constitutional prohibition on slavery and did not force fugitive slaves to return to the South (the 1850 Fugitive Slave Law provided a one thousand dollar fine or six months in jail for persons harboring runaway slaves), so that many black people worked as actual or virtual slaves in the mines. Whites often drove free black miners from the prime mining areas, taking over claims considered too lucrative for non-whites. Although there were some black-owned mining companies that became highly productive, most black men were forced to give up mining to become waiters, barbers, and general laborers. The mining c a m p s and towns of northern California formed separate churches, newspapers, and schools for blacks, although some interracial marriages did take place in the gold fields.

By 1910, California had a population of only 21,645 blacks. Between 1860 and 1910, blacks accounted for less than one per cent of the West's population. The slow increase in black population can be partly explained by the lack of availability of free public lands. Landless blacks, except for the "Exodusters," who left the South in the years between 1873 and 1879, remained largely in the South after the Civil War. There, for the most part, they did not receive the "forty acres and a mule" promised them by Northern politicians.

California's Homestead Laws offered no benefits or enticements for the masses of blacks to move to California, for under the laws of the new state black people were not given homestead rights. State Homestead Laws were passed in 1851 and again in 1860. Section Two of the 1851 law read: "Whenever any white man or female resident in this State shall desire to avail himself or herself of the benefits of this act, such person shall make a written application to the county judge of the county in which the land is situated."[1] In 1860, the California state legislature passed a concurrent resolution stating: "Resolved by the Assembly, the Senate concurring, that our Senators in Congress be instructed and our Representatives requested to use their influence to procure the passage of a law by Congress donating to each bona fide settler on the public agricultural lands within the State, being a free white person over the age of twenty-one years and a citizen of the United States; who shall have become such a homestead community of one hundred and sixty acres or more after a continuous residence and occupation thereof for five years."[2] A black man theoretically could *buy* a home or a piece of property, and some black people did. But if a white person should claim the land, the black person could not go to court to testify in his own behalf since the state's Constitution prohibited blacks from testifying in court against whites.

The following example of the injustices that occurred appeared in a black newspaper, *Pacific Appeal* (San Francisco), on May 30, 1863:

> Benjamin Berry, a black man, settled upon the southwest quarter of Section No. 12, of T. 13, N. R. 4E., has this day applied to me for advice and relief in certain matters pertaining to his claim to said land.
>
> The facts . . . appear to be that the claimant was originally a slave, born in Kentucky, taken to Missouri and then sold to a man by the name of Halloway, with whom he came to this state. This was about 1850. Here he performed services supposed to be equivalent to $3,000 and obtained his freedom. He then settled on this land, now claimed by him, erected improvements and has continued to reside there as an actual bona fide settler upon the public land. Since his settlement certain parties, taking advantage of his legal disabilities, have attempted to acquire title to the land claimed by him through the state as portion of the five hundred acre grant. It is feared that the parties now claiming adverse to Berry will proceed to eject him by an action in the state courts [Berry, as a black man, could not testify in his own behalf], and his application is made to your office for some relief and protection in his occupancy.[3]

The passage of the Perkins Bill in 1863, which gave blacks the right to testify against whites in court, eliminated some of the legal problems involved in land cases. But this change did not come about through evolution or through the good will of the white majority. It was the result of political pressure by a series of black conventions and organizations. After gaining the right to testify, the next thrust of the conventions was to abolish the provision of the 1849 Constitution which deprived black Californians of their right to vote.

As early as 1852, the Afro-American population of San Francisco organized the Franchise League to campaign for the rights to vote and testify. This group was organized after the murder of Gordan Chase, a San Francisco black barber, by a white man. The testimony of Robert Cowles, a witness, was thrown out of court because a medical examination revealed his hair to be one-sixteenth African. In 1855 and 1857, the Convention of Colored Citizens of California sent petitions to the legislature asking for the rights to vote and testify; the convention also passed resolutions against the Dred Scott Decision of 1857, which opened federal territory to slavery and denied citizenship to American blacks. In the end, black efforts at obtaining the right to vote had to wait until the Fifteenth Amendment to the United States Constitution was ratified in 1870. Nevertheless, year after year, black organizations sent petitions to the state legislature to secure passage of a voting rights bill. In 1865, the entire black male population of California organized the Executive Committee of the Colored Convention, which became a permanent organization seeking the franchise.

Black people also had to wage a fight for the privilege of riding street cars in California. It was common practice for street car employees to push black people off the cars. The famous black woman, "Mammy" Pleasant, was one such victim. Her lawyer and some white witnesses followed her as she made a second attempt to board the car; she was pushed to the street again, and immediately filed suit against the company and won damages. But segregation against black people's riding the street cars continued until a suit brought by a Mr. Brown and his daughter, Miss Charlotte Brown, in 1864 established the right of blacks to use public transportation facilities throughout California.

After 1910, blacks left the South in increasing numbers to escape tenant farming, lynchings, and institutionalized Jim Crow. The lure of jobs left vacant by recruitment of whites into the army during World War I was another factor in attracting blacks to the West. Western migration was primarily aimed at California. Between 1910 and 1920, Colorado's black population rose only from 11,453 to 12,176, and the black populations of Montana and Wyoming actually decreased. Oregon's black population increased from 1,492 in 1910 to 2,565 in 1940, while during the same period California's black population increased from 21,645 to 124,306. In 1940, then, the black population of the entire Far Western region was 170,106, with 124,306 persons in California. In California, however, Afro-Americans still made up less than two per cent of the state's total population, only a small percentage increase over 1910. By 1940, more than half of the state's black people lived in Los Angeles, a change from the migration pattern of the nineteenth century, when the black population was concentrated in the northern part of the state.

World War II and the Korean War brought about further black migrations North and West. In the 1960's, California's educational opportunities induced blacks, especially from the East, to move to "the land of milk and honey." Many young blacks in the 1950's and 1960's came immediately to California after graduating from college. Occupational opportunities increased, in part because of pressures from organizations like the NAACP and CORE. CORE pressure on downtown San Francisco stores and automobile dealers eventually made it possible for blacks to be employed as clerks and salesmen. But the demonstrations that accompanied this pressure, and the requests that stores produce records of the numbers of their black employees, met with resistance similar to that which black conventions encountered in the 1850's and 1860's. As in earlier years, some middle-class blacks condemned these efforts; they called them the work of "Communist agitators."

The black migration westward is still growing and may eventually become larger than the older black migration to the Northeast. Today black Westerners constitute 8.1 per cent of the total Western population. California is still the main destination, and it had a black population of 883,861 in 1960, with the major portion concentrated in the Los Angeles area and the remainder scattered throughout urban counties such as Alameda, San Diego, Contra Costa, and San Francisco. In 1966, 8.05 per cent of the state's public school pupils in grades kindergarten through twelve were black, according to an ethnic census, and blacks comprise the majority of the elementary school population in Oakland.

Twentieth-century black migrants, like the migrants of the Gold Rush days, have not left their racial problems behind them in the South or the East. To a large degree, California blacks lead segregated (*de facto* segregated) lives. Residential areas, school populations, and social activities tend to be drawn along black–white lines. Although theoretically there is open school enrollment, most black children cannot go to integrated primary schools. Low-income jobs do not allow blacks to purchase homes in integrated neighborhoods. In 1964, the passage of Proposition 14, an iniative abolishing the state's fair housing law, showed that a large segment of the white population of California would not sell to a black buyer even if that buyer could afford the purchase. Proposition 14 was declared unconstitutional by the United States Supreme Court in 1968.

The reaction of the black community to twentieth-century segregation initially took the form of integrationist activities. But the passage of Proposition 14 and the election of a conservative governor, Ronald Reagan, caused many young blacks to resort to violence or to turn to the concept of "black power." Many of the present Black Panthers and Black Student Union members were advocates of racial integration and were actively involved in older civil rights groups until they faced the cold reality of California's *de facto* segregation. It is fair to say that the black power movement was fathered by the failure of the liberal civil rights movement, in California as elsewhere throughout the country.

One of the most conspicuous and hard-fought demands of the black power movement in California has been for black-run black studies departments in the colleges and universities, and for black community-controlled schools. But this concept is not new in the history of education in California. In 1854, the black community of San Francisco formed a separate school. It was located on the corner of Jackson and Virginia Streets in the basement of the St. Cyprian Methodist Episcopalian Church. The basement was leased for one year at a monthly fee of fifty dollars. The teacher, Mr. J. J. Moore, the twenty-three students, and the superintendent, Mr. William Grady, all were black. In 1859, a new physical plant was built to house the students, whose number had grown to one hundred. There were 1,500 to 2,000 blacks in all of San Francisco at that time. Blacks also formed schools in Sacramento, San Jose, and other areas in the state with substantial black populations.

The first public school for black children was opened under the California statutes of 1865, Section 57, page 399, which stated:

> Children of African or Mongolian descent and Indian children not living under the care of white people should not be admitted into public schools except as provided in this act, provided that upon the written application of the parents or guardians of at least ten children to any board of trustees or board of education a separate school shall be established for the education of such children, and the education of a less number may be provided for in separate schools or in any other manner.[4]

Under this statute, Oakland's public school trustees opened a school for black children in the old Manning house located in Brooklyn, the area now called East Oakland. But, in smaller towns, there were often not enough black children to form separate schools, and consequently many black children continued to go without educations.

Black people tried to fight school segregation in the legislature, but they were not successful. They then turned to the courts, and in 1872 a convention of blacks submitted a test case to the State Supreme Court for the admission of black students into the regular public schools of California. As a result of the court's favorable decision, many black schools throughout the state were closed in 1875, and black children were supposed to attend the public schools in the areas in which they resided. But even then, black parents frequently had to take their cases to court to secure integrated educations for their children.

The case of the Wysinger family of Visalia illustrates the educational handicaps experienced by early California blacks. Mr. Wysinger was the father of six boys and two girls. He asked the county school board to establish a school for his children, and, after a fight, the board did finally open a school for black children with Sara Sanderson as teacher. When Wysinger's oldest son was ready to transfer to high school, he was refused entrance. His father had to sue the school board in the State Supreme Court before the boy could attend high school. Wysinger's story was re-enacted all over the state by black parents and black citizens' groups who wished educations for their children.

In contrast to those who sought integrated educations for their children, many black Californians in the early twentieth century desired the maintenance of black schools. This faction introduced bills into the legislature in 1913, 1914, and 1915 to create separate schools for black children. The 1915 bill was introduced by the black community of Allensworth. The people of this nearly all-black town were operating their own polytechnical school, a school similar to that in Wilberforce, Ohio. The Allensworth school was accredited, and the citizens believed that integration would reduce its quality. Allensworth was a political district with voting rights, and it was able to issue its own bonds to finance the school.

Actually, whether they desired it or not, most California blacks had integrated education only during the 1930–1950 period. This was due to the efforts of the NAACP and to the relatively small black population, which could be accommodated in the predominantly white schools without a great deal of friction. But, since the increased black migration to California that began in 1950, the trend has been toward increased *de facto* segregation in the schools.

If California did not achieve permanent school integration in the years between 1860 and 1968, how relevant is integrated education to today's black Californians? Obviously, it is irrelevant to the average black student attending an all-black school like McClymonds High School in West Oakland. School integration may be a way to end prejudice, but, of all of California's cities, only Berkeley has moved toward a fully integrated educational program. Dr. Miguel Montes, a member of the State Board of Education, believes that school integration in California is a moot point. Dr. Max Rafferty, the State Superintendent of Public Instruction, has disclosed figures which show that the number of largely segregated schools in California is still growing despite the desegregation "drives" underway in many school districts.

Integrated education may not be an issue that is relevant to today's black students, but whether or not they receive an adequate education in their black schools is. Black teachers often are not hired in ghetto area schools, even when such teachers are available and searching for employment. I belonged to a group of black teachers organized in San Francisco in 1965 to seek employment in the district. Those of our group who were eventually hired were given the status of long- or short-term substitutes, an arrangement that allowed them to be fired without redress. Most of us had to seek permanent employment in suburban districts. Dr. Ford, a black physician and member of the San Diego School Board, has observed that teaching staffs in black schools are not racially representative of the student bodies, and are less stable and usually not as qualified as those in predominantly white schools. The emphasis in black schools is too often on music, art, and drama, with too little attention given to mathematics and sciences. A well-disciplined choral or dancing group looks good to the public, but it obscures the real need of students for a scientific-business-technological preparation.

Black students, aware of these discrepancies and feeling impotent because their elders are mesmerized by educational bureaucracies, have responded with anger. If you think that black students have not properly assessed the educational situation, listen to their conversations. One black fifth-grader in a local elementary school was teasing another about the fact that his class was only half-finished with its history text. The other replied, "We're ahead in Math, though, and that's more important." A black sixth-grader said proudly, "Our teacher gives us homework every night. Your teacher hardly gives you any. How are you going to pass to junior high?"

Bussing to achieve integration is losing support among the parents of black, yellow, and brown students. Instead, minority-group parents want relevant courses taught in the present schools, by teachers who represent and are involved in the community in which the students live. And they want community control over the policies of the schools that their children attend.

The new interest in black history, culture, and power is a reaction to the racism of white culture—the racism which dominates the study of the American past, the racist laws which uphold segregation, the racist practices which maintain ghettos, the labor policies which limit occupational opportunity. These are the things that have created the current growth in support for black separatism. Those Californians who voted for Proposition 14, those who resisted school integration, have spawned the Black Panthers and the black power movement. Stokely Carmichael, like so many young blacks, is an integrationist turned cynic. The anti-white hostility of many of today's black people is really an attempt to say: "I am proud of being what I am—*black*."

Chapter VII

Conflict in the Fields: Mexican Workers in California Agri-Business

Charles Wollenberg

People of Mexican descent comprise California's largest "minority group," and for many years the United States has received more regular immigrants from Mexico than from any other country. Yet there has been little study of the role of people of Mexican descent in twentieth-century California history. Mexican-Americans have been ignored by California historians to a greater degree even than Orientals, Negroes, and Indians. Until recently, few California colleges or universities offered courses in Mexican-American history, though many of these institutions have long had extensive programs in Latin-American studies. It is little wonder, then, that contemporary "Chicano" students are demanding curricula relevant to their particular culture and experience.

In this chapter, Charles Wollenberg summarizes at least a portion of the Mexican experience in twentieth-century California: the history of Mexican and Mexican-American workers in California fields. He deals with the historical role of people of Mexican descent in the state's "agri-business" economy and discusses the long conflict between farm workers and farm owners in rural California. Mr. Wollenberg is Chairman of the History and Government Department at Laney College in Oakland and serves as the editor of this volume. His articles on the history of Mexican farm workers in California have appeared in the *Pacific Historical Review* and the *California Monthly*.

Conflict in the Fields:
Mexican Workers
in California Agri-Business

For most Californians, the Delano strike is occurring in an historical vacuum. Few people realize that the social and economic patterns that are being challenged in Delano have existed for a century, or that people of Mexican descent have been a major component of California's farm labor force for fifty years. The subject of Mexican labor in California agriculture is a vast one, and here we can treat it only in skeletal form, concentrating on an early conflict in California's fields.

It is impossible to state the precise number of people of Mexican descent living in California, let alone the number of Mexican farm laborers. The 1960 census listed about 1.4 million Californians as having "Spanish surnames." Though we know that most of these people are of Mexican origin, the designation "Spanish surname" includes persons of other Latin American and Spanish backgrounds. The term also excludes those people of Mexican descent whose family names are not of Spanish origin. To make matters worse, the census has always had difficulty counting migrants and people who have entered the United States illegally, and many Mexicans are included in both of these categories. All we can say, then, is that the 1.4 million figure provides an approximation of the Mexican and Mexican-American population of California.

If the "Spanish surname" people can be called an ethnic group, it is the largest such group in California. In 1960, it com-

This chapter is based on two articles written by Mr. Wollenberg, "Conflict in the Fields," *California Monthly* (November 1968) and "Huelga, 1929 Style: The Imperial Valley Cantaloupe Workers Strike," *Pacific Historical Review* (February 1969). Portions of those articles are reprinted here with permission.

prised nine per cent of the total population, and between 1950 and 1960 its size increased by 88 per cent, a growth rate nearly twice that of the state's total population. The census showed that about 80 per cent of the Spanish surname people in California were native-born citizens of the United States, and that more than 80 per cent lived in urban areas. Only 15 per cent of the employed men engaged in agricultural occupations.

The point of these statistics is that farm workers of Mexican descent are a minority of a minority. The great majority of California's Mexican and Mexican-American population is composed of native-born Americans who live in cities and do not engage in agriculture.

But people of Mexican origin do make up the bulk of California's unskilled farm labor force. As such, they are an indispensable part of the state's agri-business economy. "Agri-business" is a term used by both defenders and critics of California agriculture to emphasize the fact that farming is the state's biggest business, and that it is dominated by large and efficient operators. In 1959, six per cent of all farms in California controlled 75 per cent of the land under cultivation. Less than 15 per cent of the farms accounted for more than three-quarters of the total value of production and for more than four-fifths of the agricultural wages.

Agri-business has been a fact of life in California for nearly a century, and during most of that time California growers have been blessed with some ethnic or national minority group which has made up the bulk of the seasonal work force. Such workers have emigrated from societies with living standards lower than those of California. Once in California, the immigrant workers have had to contend with prejudice and discrimination. Thus they have been willing or forced to work for wages substantially lower than those paid by most non-agricultural employers.

Chinese and then Japanese filled the role of seasonal workers in nineteenth-century California. But by the second decade of the twentieth century, both Oriental groups were leaving the unskilled farm labor market, and California growers were looking for a new supply of workers. Some Filipinos, East Indians, Puerto Ricans, and Southern Negroes were imported, but, after 1910, the greatest source of new labor was Mexico.

There had been substantial immigration from Mexico to California during the Gold Rush, but, by the middle 1850's, prejudice and the declining supply of gold had brought this movement to a halt. Not until the Mexican Revolution of 1910 did the northern migration resume. In that year, the partisans of Francisco I. Madero challenged the dictatorship of Porfirio Díaz, and a full-scale social revolution exploded over Mexico. The ensuing decade of political chaos and violence broke down social and institutional restraints that had held people to a particular hacienda or village. The Mexican economy was one of the victims of the revolution, and until the 1920's poverty was even more widespread than usual. Thus conditions in Mexico were forcing people to leave their homeland and cross the northern border.

At the same time, the labor shortage in California fields was becoming acute. World War I created an increased demand for California's agricultural goods, but it also created a labor crisis. Able-bodied men were drafted into the armed services, and immigration from Europe was drastically cut by war-time conditions. Growers in California and Texas, indeed throughout the country, demanded that the government allow Mexicans to enter the United States as temporary, seasonal workers. As a result, Mexicans crossed the border virtually without restraint during the war years.

By 1919, many California growers already had become dependent on Mexican labor. This dependency increased during the 1920's, for Mexico now proved to be as good a source of cheap labor as China and Japan had been in the nineteenth century. The immigration legislation of the early 1920's excluded Asians and established quotas for Europeans, but no such restrictions were placed upon immigration from Mexico or the rest of the Western hemisphere. Mexican immigrants were required to pay a small "head tax" and were subject to "qualitative" restrictions, such as the requirement that they show evidence that they would not become recipients of public welfare or relief. But most Mexicans who entered California during the 1920's did not bother with taxes or qualitative restrictions; they simply crossed the border illegally. Before 1924, there were less than one hundred men patrolling the American side of the U.S.-Mexican border, and even the establishment of the Border Patrol in 1924 did not raise the total above five hundred.

One of the first major agricultural regions in California to become dependent on Mexican labor was the Imperial Valley, which is adjacent to the Mexican border in the southeastern part of the state. During the first decade of the twentieth century, extensive irrigation projects opened Imperial desert land to cultivation. The original agricultural pioneers of those years utilized American Indian, "white," and Oriental labor, but as early as 1920 Mexicans were dominating the valley's harvest work. By the middle 1920's, a process had occurred in the Imperial Valley that would be repeated again and again throughout rural California —the immigrant Mexican laborers had become resident laborers of Mexican descent. In 1928, approximately one third of the 60,000 permanent residents of Imperial County were people of Mexican origin. Virtually all economically active Mexicans living in the county were field workers. Some of them spent a few weeks each year in other agricultural regions of California and the Southwest, but they lived most of the year in Imperial Valley towns and worked most of the year in Imperial Valley fields.

The chief employers of agricultural labor in the valley were large landholders, either individuals or corporations that owned or leased large holdings. Such growers needed big work crews, and, rather than take the trouble of hiring great numbers of workers directly, they used the services of labor contractors. The contractors were often men of Mexican descent who organized work crews, collected wages from employers, and distributed the money to the workers. The workers sometimes complained that the contractors did not pay the full wages as promised.

Because the valley had many harvests, the annual income of Imperial workers was probably higher than that of farm workers in other areas of the state. Nevertheless, a detailed survey made in 1928 by Dr. Paul S. Taylor disclosed the fact that most of the valley's Mexican population lived in one- or two-room shacks that lacked indoor plumbing of any kind.[1]

There was a deep social separation between the Imperial Valley's Mexican and "Anglo" communities. Most people of Mexican descent lived in their own *barrios* or neighborhoods, usually located on the outskirts of town. Elementary school lines were drawn so that virtually all children of Mexican descent attended segregated schools.

The Mexican community had its own structure and leadership. An important institution was the *mutualista* or mutual aid society. The valley's two *mutualistas* provided their members with small medical and unemployment payments in times of need, and they also handled general charity within the Mexican community. The *mutualistas* sponsored celebrations of Mexican holidays, dances, and showings of Mexican movies. There were also Mexican cafes and pool halls to provide less formal social activities. Spanish-language newspapers were available from Mexicali and Los Angeles, and the Mexican vice-consul at Calexico served the valley's Spanish-speaking population as a representative to official agencies of the Mexican, United States, and California governments.

By 1928, then, Mexican workers had become an integral if not an equal part of the Imperial Valley's economic system, and organizations representing growers acted energetically to protect this labor source. In early 1928, legislation was introduced in Congress to apply the strict 1924 immigration quota system to Mexico and the rest of the Western hemisphere. Imperial County's Western Growers Protective Association joined with similar organizations in California, Arizona, and Texas to fight the bill. The association's executive secretary, a Calexico banker, spent six weeks in Washington lobbying against the measure, which was finally bottled up in committee.

Meanwhile, in the spring of 1928, the Mexican community of the Imperial Valley had given birth to a labor union of agricultural workers, patterned after similar organizational efforts by Mexicans in the Los Angeles region. The union seems to have been started by some of the leaders of the *mutualistas* with co-operation from the consulate at Calexico. Before the harvest of the valley's most valuable crop, the cantaloupe, the union sent letters to major growers, asking for small improvements in wages and working conditions. The letters were polite and contained no threat of a strike. Nevertheless, the growers ignored the letters, and in some cases sent them back unopened.

On Monday, May 7, 1928, the first day of extensive harvesting, groups of workers began what appear to have been spontaneous and unorganized walk-outs in some of the cantaloupe fields of the Imperial Valley. As the word of the walk-outs spread, more and more people joined the movement. By Wednesday, May 9, most harvest work stopped. Even the valley's Anglo press, which was trying to play down the importance of the strike, admitted that two to three thousand Mexican workers were staying off the job.

The growers threatened to replace the strikers with workers imported from Texas and Arizona. They also called upon the law enforcement officials of Imperial County to support the cause of the employers. The response of these officials was reflected in this statement by the district attorney: "Imperial Valley melon growers have millions of dollars invested in a highly perishable crop, and every resource of law enforcement machinery is to be used in harvesting that crop."[2]

County Sheriff Charles Gillett claimed that "Mexicans are excitable and if idle will gather into groups to their own detriment as well as hindering work in the fields."[3] Given these premises, the sheriff's tactics were obvious: he would see to it that Mexicans in the Imperial Valley neither "remained idle" nor "gathered into groups." All "congregations of foreigners" in the valley were prohibited for the duration of the emergency. Mexican workers who gathered on street corners were arrested. Even a delegation of strikers which had been invited to discuss the situation with the district attorney was jailed as they walked to the county courthouse. Union offices were closed, as were cafes and pool halls that served a Mexican clientele. The sheriff claimed to have a "secret service" operating in Mexican neighborhoods to find out who the agitators and troublemakers really were. On May 13, 1928, a Mexican newspaper distributor in the valley town of Brawley was arrested for allegedly writing on his billboard, "Forty-eight Mexicans in jail—What for?—Nothing."

By Monday, May 14, most workers were back in the fields. The strike had been shattered by the effective action of growers and law enforcement officials. By Friday, May 18, the 1928 cantaloupe harvest was proceeding at record pace.

Compared in scope or drama with other conflicts in California fields—the Wheatland strike of 1913, the class warfare of the 1930's, or the Delano *huelga* of our own time—the Imperial Valley cantaloupe workers' strike is a minor incident. But it is an important chapter in California labor history, for it seems to be the first successful attempt by farm workers of Mexican origin to stall, even for a short time, the entire harvest of an important agricultural region of the state.

As such, the strike shattered some of the stereotypes that had been attached to Mexican agricultural workers. A study conducted in the Imperial Valley in 1928 revealed that most growers regarded their workers as "bovine and tractable individuals," people who passively and happily went about their modest jobs.[4] One California rancher believed that a Mexican worker "never causes trouble except when he indulges in intoxicants."

Given such attitudes, many growers could explain the strike only as the work of outside agitators or radicals who had stirred up the contented workers. One employer claimed that "agitators or Communists, or whatever they are, have come with their comrade stuff and with threats have intimidated the workers." The county sheriff said that the strike was caused by "reds and radicals." A *Los Angeles Times* headline read, "IWW members are in back of the movement."[5]

The record seems to indicate that these charges are without foundation. The official report of the State Bureau of Industrial

Relations regarding the strike concluded that there was no evidence pointing to professional agitators or members of radical groups as organizers of the work stoppages. The press coverage of the legal hearings and trials of those arrested in connection with the strike gives no indication that the district attorney attempted to prove that the defendants were members of radical organizations or non-residents of the Imperial Valley.

There are, of course, many parallels between the Imperial Valley strike and the current conflict in Delano. Perhaps the most important similarity is that in both cases the great majority of striking workers have been California residents rather than temporary migrants who regularly return to Mexico. During the forty years that have elapsed between these two labor struggles, the bargaining power of these resident farm workers of Mexican descent has been continually undermined by events and by the presence of alternative labor sources.

The depression of the 1930's caused a drastic decline in agricultural prices and wages. By 1933, Mexican workers in the vegetable and berry fields near Los Angeles were receiving as little as nine cents an hour. At the same time, large numbers of Anglo migrants, the "Okies" and "Arkies," were forced into the unskilled farm labor market in competition with workers of Mexican descent. There were massive agricultural strikes during the 1930's, many of them carried out by Mexican workers, but there were very few meaningful victories. The immigration statistics of the 1930's indicate that there was a net outflow of people from the United States to Mexico, some of them victims of forced "repatriations" managed by relief authorities in California counties.

World War II brought prosperity to most Californians, but it did little to improve the bargaining position of resident farm workers of Mexican origin. For it was during the war that the Bracero Program was initiated, and thus California growers received a government guarantee of cheap migrant labor from Mexico. The *braceros,* or "strong-armed ones," came to California as the result of a bilateral agreement between the Mexican and

American governments which allowed Mexican field laborers to work in the United States for limited periods of time. The United States government was obligated to assure that the temporary migrants received fair treatment, adequate living and working conditions, minimum wages (which varied according to time and place), and various other protections and benefits.

In theory, the Bracero Program was an emergency measure to be terminated when the war-time labor shortage ended. In fact, the program continued under various guises in the late 1940's and was formally re-established and strengthened when Congress passed Public Law 78 in 1951. In terms of numbers, the peak was reached in 1956, when more than 400,000 braceros legally entered the United States, more than a third of whom came to California.

Along with the braceros, there was an even larger post-war immigration of Mexican workers who crossed the border illegally. Although it is impossible to know the precise number of these "wetbacks," in 1951 an estimated 500,000 entered the United States, and, again, about a third of them came to California.

These immigrations from Mexico, both official and illegal, had a profound effect on resident farm workers of Mexican origin. To put it simply, wages were kept down and bargaining positions remained weak as long as a supply of temporary migrant labor from Mexico was available.

The first major restriction of that supply came in 1953, when the American government launched "Operation Wetback," a concerted campaign to prevent further illegal immigration from Mexico. By 1956, the wetback traffic had been substantially cut. For a time, the slack was taken up by increased numbers of braceros, but in 1964, twenty-two years after it had begun as a temporary war-time measure, the Bracero Program itself was terminated. In 1965, a new immigration law for the first time in United States history placed numerical limits on immigrants from Western hemisphere nations (in 1968, a total of 120,000 for the entire hemisphere). In recent months, the United Farm Workers Organizing Committee and other supporters of the Delano strike have called for severe restrictions on "green carders," Mexican nationals with official U.S. permits to work in the United States (though not under the provisions of an international agreement such as the Bracero Program).

The increasing restriction of immigration from Mexico has improved the bargaining position of resident agricultural workers and thus has increased labor costs for California growers. This, in turn, has speeded up the process of agricultural mechanization, a process already well advanced in California. As the availability of cheap labor diminishes, farmers find it profitable to invest in machines, particularly for harvest work. The machines, of course, reduce the number of unskilled laborers needed in California fields, although they also create opportunities for some workers to move into higher-paying jobs.

In the midst of this contradictory situation, the United Farm Workers Organizing Committee, led by César Chavez, has carried on its now-famous Delano strike. I assume that we shall talk more about the Delano movement during the question-and-answer period, but here it is important to point out that while the strikers have taken advantage of the improved bargaining position created by increasing immigration restriction, they are threatened by the long-term trend of agricultural mechanization. Thus, although the UFWOC has won collective bargaining contracts from several wine-grape growers and already is the most successful farm labor union in California history, the eventual outcome of the Delano conflict is very much in doubt.

But one thing is certain—the three interrelated processes of restriction of Mexican immigration, possible unionization of resident farm workers, and agricultural mechanization are revolutionizing California agriculture. Social and economical relationships between growers and workers that have existed for a century in rural California are changing. The shape of future labor relations in the agri-business economy is not yet clear. But we can predict that change will be painful and that the conflict in California fields is by no means at an end.

Selected Questions and Answers

Q. "In the Salinas Valley there used to be a tremendous number of agricultural workers used during the lettuce harvests, and now there is a very small number. The same thing is true of the cotton fields in the San Joaquin Valley."

A. "Automation or mechanization, in itself, is a neutral process. Its effect on the workers depends, at least in part, on the workers' power. If they are well organized, they can demand a share of the increased profits in the form of higher wages, retraining programs, and early retirement benefits. It is reported that something like this has happened with farm workers in Hawaii. On the other hand, if the workers have little or no power, mechanization can be a disaster. Apparently, in Mississippi and Alabama, mechanization of cotton farming has put thousands of black people out of work without giving them a share of the profits created by the machines. We now see reports on television and in the newspapers of dispossessed sharecroppers and cotton pickers who are so poor that they cannot afford to buy federal food stamps."

Q. "Are there no growers who have any feelings? Are they all bad?"

A. "I suppose growers are as good or as bad as anyone else. Some, for example, have made a real effort to provide good housing for their workers; others house workers in places that are unfit for animals. But there are limits to what an individual grower can do, particularly if he is a small or medium-sized operator. If he increases labor costs too much, he cannot compete and survive. It is significant that the first growers to sign union contracts with the Delano movement were large corporations, DiGiorgio and Schenley, whose grape-growing operations were very small parts of their total business activities; thus, increased costs for field labor had little over-all effect on their profits. This is true of most wineries, and it is one of the reasons that the union has had an easier time with wine-grape growers than with table-grape growers."

Q. "What is your assessment of the Delano union organization up to this point in history, and what about the future?"

A. "The Delano strike is by far the most successful agricultural strike in California history. The union has been able to survive for three years, and it actually has won collective bargaining contracts with DiGiorgio, Schenley, Christian Brothers, Almadén, and others. Although the union is primarily Mexican-American, it has also won the support of some Filipino and Anglo workers; in fact, it was Filipino workers who began the Delano walk-outs. And, of course, the Delano movement has created a significant and nationally-known leader in César Chavez.

"But in spite of all this, the UFWOC has barely scratched the surface. The overwhelming majority of farm workers in California are not unionized. It seems to me that this will continue to be true until farm workers obtain legislation giving them federal protection to bargain collectively under the jurisdiction of the National Labor Relations Board. Most workers in other industries have had such protection since the 1930's. If this kind of legislation for farm workers were passed by Congress, it is possible that the Delano union, as the existing farm workers' union which has won some success and has gained great publicity, would spread rapidly throughout California and the rest of the Southwest."

Q. "Do you know the actual outside groups that are now supporting the Delano strike? Can you enumerate the different kinds of groups?"

A. "There are a great many such groups. In fact, the ability of the Delano movement to gain so much outside support has been one of the reasons for its relative success.

"Certainly support from other unions has been important. Early in the strike, Walter Reuther visited Delano and pledged considerable financial support from the United Auto Workers. Other unions and county central labor councils throughout California have contributed money and supplies. Unions have given powerful support to the boycott tactics of the Delano strikers. However, in the collective bargaining election at DiGiorgio, the

Delano union had to compete against the Teamsters Union, which also tried to organize the farm workers. Faced with this powerful opposition, Chavez and his followers affiliated with the AFL-CIO. They won the election, and AFL-CIO support has been important ever since.

"Also, there has been considerable support from Mexican-American organizations throughout the state. I suppose that, in some respects, Chavez for Mexican-Americans has played a role similar to that played by Martin Luther King in the black protest movement. Chavez as a leader and the Delano strike as a cause have provided rallying points for a wide range of Mexican-American organizations and viewpoints. A spark of militancy has been lit that isn't about to go out.

"There has also been great support among 'white liberals,' whatever they are. The Delano strike came just in time for many whites. Their social consciences had been awakened by the civil rights movement, but, by 1965 or 1966, the black power phase was forcing whites out of the movement. Delano was a good cause, and whites were not turned away. Many young white people became directly involved in marches, boycotts, and picket lines; some have done staff work in Delano. Older liberals have contributed money.

"All of this had a political effect on the Democratic Party, since white liberals, organized labor, and Mexican-Americans all have some influence on that party's affairs in California. John Kennedy was perhaps the first national politician to recognize the importance of the Mexican-American vote, and the 'Viva Kennedy' campaign of 1960 was very successful in California. It was no accident that Robert Kennedy identified himself closely with the Delano movement, and the feeling was mutual.

"Finally, we shouldn't forget support from religious groups. Some liberal sectors of the Protestant denominations, including of course the group known as the 'Migrant Ministry,' have allied themselves closely with the Delano strike. Organized Catholic support was a bit slower in coming, but come it did, particularly during and after the famous farm workers' march on Sacramento in the spring of 1966. That march took place under the banner of the Virgin of Guadalupe. Growing Church support for the Delano strike seems to be part of a rather belated effort by the Church in California to identify itself with its Mexican and Mexican-American parishoners."

Q. "Are farm workers covered by the minimum wage law?"

A. "Yes, the federal minimum wage law does now apply to most farm workers, although the wage is a good deal lower than that for other industries. Also, the state minimum wage law applies to women and children."

Q. "In my part of the state, they have tried to get domestic workers to work in the fields, but they haven't found any. Domestic workers won't do that kind of work."

A. "Well, many of the so-called Mexican workers actually are 'domestic workers.' They are people of Mexican descent who have been born and raised in California and are American citizens. I suppose you really mean 'white' or 'Anglo' workers. While there are some Anglos doing field labor, historically this work has been done largely by ethnic minorities, and historically wages have been much lower than those in other industries. It seems to me that in order really to test the availability of labor, you must be willing to offer wages that are competitive with other, particularly urban, employers."

Q. "All the people around our community are family farmers, small farmers. They pay their workers as much as they can, but if they paid more they would be out of business. My family has invested about $400,000 in a farm, and the men put in about sixteen hours a day, and yet they do not have as much spending money as the man who works for them. They just can't compete with industry in wages."

A. "It is true that a single farm, particularly a family farm, cannot suddenly raise wages, dramatically better working conditions, and still stay in business. Any meaningful change will have to affect the entire industry, the whole agri-business economy of the state and the nation. Even so, such an industry-wide change might still favor the large producer and drive the small and middle-sized farmer out of business by making labor and equipment costs so high that only the big operator could afford them. However, we must face the question of whether it is proper to support and defend the interests of one group, the family-sized farmers, by keeping another group, the unskilled field workers, in poverty. And it is clear that most families of farm workers subsist on incomes well below the levels set by the federal government to define 'poverty.' The question of the future of the family farm goes well beyond the problem of farm labor. We must also look at public policies regarding agricultural subsidies, distribution of irrigation water, and control of large wholesalers and retailers. And, of course, we must consider the effect of tax laws of both the state and the federal governments. Those interested in this subject might want to read some of the works of Dr. Paul S. Taylor of the University of California. He is a defender of the family farm and also an advocate of better wages and working conditions for farm workers."

Q. "Weren't there a great many reforms attempted or at least proposed during the thirties?"

A. "Yes. As I have pointed out, during the depression large numbers of Anglo workers, particularly immigrants from Oklahoma and the other states of the southern Midwest, entered the farm labor market in California. They suffered greatly, and their plight attracted the attention of reformers. John Steinbeck's books, particularly *The Grapes of Wrath,* stimulated great public sympathy. Just prior to World War II, a Senate sub-committee headed by Senator La Follette held hearings in California and recommended many substantial reforms. The state government under Governor Olsen also was considering reforms. Then the outbreak of war not only distracted people's attention, but also helped to solve the economic problems of the 'Okies' and 'Arkies,' who were drafted or found work in defense industries. The clamor for reform of farm labor died out, and most of the recommendations and proposals were never passed into law. During the thirties, the Anglo immigrants from the Midwest found themselves in a social and economic position usually reserved in

California for ethnic minorities. Not only were they forced to do harvest labor, but also terms like 'Okie' and 'Arkie' took on connotations similar to 'nigger' and 'greaser.' It was almost as if a white, Anglo-Saxon, Protestant ethnic minority had been created, for the Okies were subjected to the same kinds of prejudice, discrimination, and exploitation that minority groups have suffered in America. However, when the war solved the problems of most of the Anglo farm workers, the demand for reform quieted, and it was not revived in a major way until the civil rights movement touched America's social conscience and raised the issue of racial prejudice. In the meantime, people of Mexican descent continued to suffer many of the same problems that had plagued the Okies."

Chapter VIII

Afro-Americans and Mexican-Americans: The Politics of Coalition

Mervyn M. Dymally

A Chicano Response

Samuel Soto Ortega

Nowhere has the powerlessness of ethnic minorities in California life been more apparent than in the state's politics. Minority groups have been under-represented at all levels of the political system for most of the state's history. However, in recent years, great efforts have been made to change this situation. One of the leaders in this campaign has been the Honorable Mervyn M. Dymally, State Senator from Los Angeles County. Senator Dymally is the only black member of California's upper house, where he served as Chairman of the Social Welfare Committee and is a member of the Education Committee. He is a former teacher and Assemblyman and was a founder of the National Conference of Black Elected Officials.

In this chapter, Senator Dymally argues for a political coalition of Afro-American and Mexican-American voters. Following the Senator's presentation, the concept of a black and brown coalition is discussed by Samuel Ortega, Director of the Sacramento Concilio. The Concilio is a broadly-based community council of Mexican-Americans in the Sacramento area; thus, Mr. Ortega speaks with an intimate knowledge of the problems of California's urban Spanish-speaking population. His comments go far beyond the specific proposals made by Senator Dymally to a critique of the lecture series from which this book evolved and a general discussion of the status of the Mexican-American in contemporary California.

Afro-Americans and Mexican-Americans: The Politics of Coalition

Mervyn M. Dymally

Somebody on the inside once said that politics is the art of the possible; but for the black and brown outsider in America, politics has been the art of the impossible.

It has been the art of the impossible because it has been the art of trying to make fundamental changes in a political system by using structures and instruments that were designed to perpetuate the system.

It has been the art of the impossible because it has been the art of trying to make a social revolution with moderate tools that were invented to prevent social revolution.

It has been the art of the impossible because of the nature of politics, which is the art of making some things impossible for outsiders. And because of the black and brown man's situation, which cannot be changed unless all things are made possible, the black and brown man's role in American politics continues to be impossible.

Because of the black and brown man's situation, which is radical by any definition, and because of the nature of American politics, which is moderate to conservative by any definition, the black and brown man in America has been condemned to seek radical ends within a political framework that was designed to prevent sudden and radical social and economic changes.

For almost a hundred years now, these outsiders of America have been squirming within the halters of this maddening dilemma. During this period, some representatives of the outsiders have made striking gains as *individuals* within the councils of the insiders. But black and brown people as a group have not been able to change their status or their social or economic conditions with the old political instruments. And the question we must grapple with now is whether or not it will ever be possible to achieve fundamental social and economic changes by the practice of politics, as defined by the insiders.

The question now—and the question is radical because the times are radical, and because our situation is radical—is whether or not politics is relevant to our contemporary crisis, which cannot be resolved without political programs of a depth and dimension never before attempted in America.

Is the old politics—the politics of deals and trades and patronage, the politics of place and privilege and individual advancement—relevant to the issues of bread for the millions and housing and education for the poor? Is politics relevant to black and brown reality?

Beyond all that, beyond the specific problems of black and brown people, we must ask whether politics is relevant to white people. Is it relevant to the emptiness, hysteria, and unresolved social and economic problems of the white community? Can the old politics create white people who will not need racial scapegoats to solve their social, economic, and racial anxieties?

Watts, Newark, and Detroit put these questions on the agenda of American life. In a very real sense, these rebellions were devastating critiques of the American way of politics. In rebellion, these people of America have said that they are voting more and enjoying it less. In rebellion, these people have said that politics in America has failed them, and that it is necessary now to create a new politics, a kind of politics that can address itself to the real problem of this profoundly *racist* society.

It is against this background that we must view the question of the Afro-American and the Mexican-American, and the politics of coalition. And in the light of these events, and the history these events reflect, we must say frankly that minority people have no role in contemporary politics.

Black and brown people are the outsiders, the disinherited, of the American political system. As human beings, they live outside white America in numerous black and brown colonies. As voters and political persons, they inhabit the margins on the periphery of the system. But they have crucially affected the system by their presence on the periphery—they have acted on the system from a distance. Indeed, one might say that the political history of America is a series of approaches to and withdrawals from the pressing reality of the minorities on the margins. The role of the black and brown man *outside* American politics, then, has been the dual role of an instrument for insiders, and of a protagonist living and working on the outside of the whole political system.

In considering this dual role, we have to deal with what J. D. B. Miller, the political theorist, calls "the politics of the center and the circumference." We have to deal, in other words, with a quasi-colonial relationship. As Dr. Kenneth Clark noted in his book, *Dark Ghetto,* "the dark ghettos are social, political, educational, and—above all—economic colonies. Their inhabitants are subject people, victims of the greed, cruelty, insensitivity, guilt, and fear of their masters." What I am concerned to emphasize here is that these colonies are controlled politically from the outside. Ultimate policy-making power lies in the hands of people who have their own representatives, some of them black, some of them brown, on the spot, with power to see that the will of the white center is obeyed in the black and brown circumference. "Black people and white people," as Gunnar Myrdal has said in *An American Dilemma,* "deal with each other, like two foreign countries, through the medium of plentipotentiaries." We must note also that the inhabitants of the circumference do not deal with each other directly.

I say this with bluntness to emphasize the fact that when we talk about coalition politics we are not talking about ordinary politics, and we are not talking about ordinary politics because the American political system has not created a single social community in which the reciprocal rules of politics apply. Conventional politics cannot solve this problem, because conventional politics is *a part* of the problem.

It is a part of the problem because the political system is the major bulwark of racism in America, in both the Democratic and Republican parties, not to mention the American Independent Party. It is a part of the problem in the sense that the political system is structured to repel fundamental social and economic changes. We hear a great deal about the deficiencies, real or imagined, of certain minority leaders, but not enough attention, it seems to me, is paid to the framework within which they operate. That framework prevents radical growth or innovation—as indeed it was *designed* to do.

What we have to deal with here is what Arthur Schlesinger, Jr., called *the paradox of power*—the fact that power within the system is necessary to do certain things, but that power within the system makes it impossible to do most things. John F. Kennedy was no political novice when he became President, but he didn't realize, Schlesinger tells us, how beautifully the government structure was organized to prevent anything from happening.

From the very beginning, the American political structure has been beautifully organized to keep anything from happening. We need not deal with the theory that the Constitutional Convention was a conspiracy against the revolutionary ideals of the Declaration of Independence. But it is obvious from a cursory examination of the Constitution that the founding fathers were animated by a desire to protect property and privilege from sudden social experiment. Thomas Jefferson, a large and wealthy slaveowner, protested the anti-people biases of the new government, but he did not prevail. The theory of checks and balances, for example, is based on the theory that privilege must be protected from the people. An additional safeguard was the two-party system, which was designed, in part, to filter out radicalism, and to force dissent to express itself within moderate channels. Insofar as the minority person is concerned, one can say of the two parties what a political insider said to Lord Bryce: "They are like two bottles of the same size, the same color and the same shape, with the same label—both of them empty."

The criticism I make here of politics in America could be extended to most political structures, certainly most political structures in the West. Governments cannot operate without support, and this means in practice that they must identify with certain interests in society. In America, the government has usually identified with the interests of big white people.

Nothing illustrates this better than the central events in the political history of the black and brown man in California. Two hundred years ago, men of the black and brown races entered California as free men. Today, they are struggling to regain that freedom, somehow lost during the years when California became the richest and most powerful state in a nation that is the richest and most powerful the world has ever seen. And today, when Afro-Americans and Mexican-Americans talk of coalition, of joint efforts to gain equal opportunities in an economic struggle that has all but overwhelmed them, they can look back with pride to a heritage as early settlers in California. As they populate the ghettos and *barrios* of stagnating cities, they can look back to the time when the blacks and the browns were first citizens of a green and promising land and shared equally in the responsibilities and rewards of a fledgling state.

Afro-Americans played an important role in settling California. Sonora, Sinaloa, and Baja California included many part-Africans among their Spanish-speaking residents. In 1790, the population of Baja California included 844 Spanish-speaking persons; more than 20 per cent of these were mulattos, and almost half were *castas,* persons of unclassified mixed ancestry. The Portola expedition, which founded San Diego and Monterey and explored the coast, included at least one mulatto soldier, Juan Antonio Coronel, and several mulatto mule drivers. The Juan Bautista de Anza expedition of 1775 included seven mulatto soldiers of a total of twenty-nine, or nearly one in four. Over-all, one in five of the Spanish-speaking settlers and soldiers in California in the 1790's was of African or part-African background. All of the early African pioneers in California, whether soldiers or civilian settlers, were free men and women.

Of the first forty-six *pobladores* or settlers of Los Angeles in 1781, twenty-six were African or part-African. Of the remainder, one was a Chinese from Manila, two were "Español," and the rest were Indian or part-Indian. According to Dr. Jack D. Forbes of the Far West Laboratory, "Early Los Angeles was thoroughly integrated since house lots were distributed to the settlers without reference to racial characteristics." Also racially mixed were the newly-settled towns of Santa Barbara, Monterey, and San Francisco.

The first rancher in the San Fernando Valley was Francisco Reyes, a mulatto, who served as mayor of Los Angeles from 1793 to 1795. The first rancher in the area east and southeast of Los Angeles was Manuel Nieto, a soldier who was the son of a black man and an "Español" woman.

One of the most successful Afro-Americans was William Alexander Leidesdorff, a mulatto, who arrived late in the Mexican period, became a Mexican citizen in 1844, and acquired a land grant in the Sacramento Valley. In 1844, he went to San Francisco, where, according to H. H. Bancroft, the California historian, he was not only one of San Francisco's most prominent businessmen, but a member of the council, treasurer, and member of the school committee, taking an active part in local politics. He died, still a young man, in 1845, one year before "decendants of Africans" were legally stigmatized in California.

Tens of thousands of descendants of those early Afro-Americans are still living in California, either as members of the Mexican-American community or of the English-speaking white population. Once more in our history, the times demand that the Afro-American and the Mexican-American come together to solve a continuing crisis.

The central cities of this increasingly urban nation are not only threatened with collapse; they are, in fact, collapsing, in large part because of the fiscal drain of the ghetto and the *barrio*. As a consequence, what we are confronted with in the civil rights and farm struggles is no longer a problem for the Afro-American or the Mexican-American alone, but for the whole society. Urban trouble is a challenge to our social structure. There is despair on our streets and farms, and it cries out for bold, statesman-like resolution.

A little later, I will mention what I consider to be a hopeful trend toward an active political coalition between black and brown. But first, let us take a look at a program of seven basic goals for which a coalition should strive.

    1. *To restore full employment as rapidly as possible, and to maintain it thereafter, for all persons able and willing to work, and for all whom adequate training and education would make able and willing.* This means an unemployment rate below three per cent by early 1970. Fully 40 per cent of all U.S. poverty is directly attributable to inadequate employment opportunity, and involuntary unemployment is corrosive to the human spirit.

    2. *To assure adequate incomes for those employed.* About 20 per cent of all U.S. poverty is found among the working poor and their dependents, people who receive sub-standard incomes. The treatment of this problem depends primarily upon federal legislation.

    3. *To guarantee a minimum level of income for all those who cannot be gainfully employed.* About 40 per cent of all U.S. poverty is found among those who cannot work because of age or other disabling factors. More than 13 per cent of all U.S. poverty is found among families headed by women who cannot work. Until, under federal auspices, we achieve such a guaranteed annual income, there should be immediate and vast improvements in all Social Security, welfare, and job training programs, with much larger federal participation.

    4. *To wipe out the slum ghettos and* barrios *and provide a decent home for every American family within a decade.* Bad housing is both cause and consequence of poverty. It breeds resentment and unrest. Housing, on a scale matching the need, would also make the largest single contribution to job creation in the face of job displacement by technological trends elsewhere in the economy. It would accent the types of jobs suitable for those most vulnerable to unemployment.

    5. *To provide, for all Americans, modern medical care to the limits of their needs, and educational opportunity to the limits of their abilities and ambitions, at costs within their means.* The shortage of personnel and facilities that became apparent upon

the enactment of Medicare (which helps only the aged portion of the population) speaks for itself. Many schools and children in our great cities are in need of great help.

6. *To overcome other manifestations of neglect in the public sector by purifying our air and waters, and by bringing our transportation systems and natural resources development into line with the needs of a growing population and an expanding economy.* This, too, would provide the types of jobs most suited to reducing unemployment. Along with housing, it would immensely improve the living conditions even of those who already enjoy "freedom from want" in a more limited sense.

7. *To unite sustained full employment with sustained full production and high economic growth.* This is essential in order that "freedom from want" may be achieved not by robbing Peter to pay Paul, but under conditions that will bring progress to all.

These goals are basic. If we turn our backs on them, we will be surrendering to the politics of fear and frustration.

Even though unemployment, according to official figures, is now down to around four per cent, white as well as black and brown workers in this technological, automated economy still dread the possibility that they might lose their jobs. As long as a psychology of scarcity and depression is abroad in the land, just so long will there be a tendency for the organized to be wary of the unorganized, for the white employed to feel threatened by the black and brown unemployed and underemployed.

The same is true of small homeowners. As long as the blacks and the browns are denied free and reasonable access to private housing markets, as long as low and moderately priced housing in general is scarce, just so long will the white small homeowners view minority movements seeking decent and human habitations as threats to their security.

In 1954, the Supreme Court ruled that separate or segregated education is, by definition, inferior. We thought that this represented the removal of the major roadblock to full citizenship and real participation in the mainstream of American life for all people. The way seemed clear for every citizen to develop to the full potential of his ability. But the law of the land was not enforced. Today, fifteen years later, only 13 per cent of the black children in the South attend integrated schools. Over 50 per cent of the children in New York City are Afro-American or Puerto Rican-American, and 90 per cent of them attend segregated schools. The same is true of the nation's capital, Washington, D.C. The white population of Philadelphia declined from 51 per cent in 1961 to 43 per cent in 1965. White enrollment in Detroit has dropped by 9.2 per cent in the last five years.

Most important, however, is the fact that the children left behind in the segregated schools are not being taught. A recent survey of the reading levels in urban segregated schools shows that, in some areas, almost 87 per cent of the children are reading below grade level. In 1954, the year of the great court decision, 50 per cent were reading below grade level. At this rate, by 1970, all of the children in the ghetto schools in urban areas will be "underachievers."

Colleges and universities are unconsciously, or perhaps consciously, discriminating against low-income and minority (black and brown) students by continuing to use testing requirements which favor students from middle-class, old, white American families. The Mexican-American and Afro-American communities have already started reform programs directed against the colleges and universities for this shameful exclusion of minority students from our institutions of higher learning.

What about housing? Thirty-four million Americans are officially designated "poor." By 1970, nearly 80 per cent of our population will live in urban areas. More significantly, by 1970, more than 50 per cent of the black and brown people will live in the North, West, and Southwest, mainly in inner-city areas. This means that the problem of slum housing is very much the black and brown man's problem. More and more people are migrating to the cities in search of jobs, housing, decent lives. But when they arrive, they will join their urban brothers in being denied access to jobs, housing, and decent lives. We must develop programs which will do away with poor people's feelings of uselessness and helplessness. There is only one answer: the federal government must accept its responsibilities. Recent testimony before the U.S. Senate has shown that federal housing programs have never really been used for the benefit of the masses of people and, in fact, have perpetuated segregation.

Let's briefly review the employment situation. The statistics are familiar to all of us, but they paint only half the picture. The other half, the *solutions,* will require money and determination. The question of financing is not the major problem. There is a problem far deeper and greater in scope, and that is the attitude of the government, as well as private industry, toward its responsibility to the millions of poor and unemployed citizens in the Afro-American and Mexican-American communities in this country. It is necessary here to cite the following statistics: in August, 1955, the white national unemployment rate was 4.1 per cent; the non-white unemployment rate was 7.7 per cent, the traditional level of almost twice as many unemployed minority group members as whites. Currently, minority unemployment is even worse. The gap continues to widen. Among young men of eighteen to twenty-four, the national rate of unemployment is five times as high for non-whites as for whites. In addition to the problem of unemployment is the hidden factor of equal pay for equal work—Afro-Americans and Mexican-Americans with Ph.D.'s, for example, make an average of four thousand dollars a year less than white Ph.D.'s. Unemployment is a national problem and it must be dealt with on a national level.

What about welfare? The system of public welfare fosters dependency and denies the basic human rights of the poor. In many cases, once you become a welfare recipient, you lose most of your rights and have no means by which to assert those that remain except through the good graces of the social worker. Programs are needed to encourage competitive activities among the minorities and the poor. I support the proposal for a guaranteed income maintenance system or a negative income tax because it guarantees money as a *right* to those who are unable to support themselves. But this system alone will not affect the economic system that now exists in this country. We must challenge business, industry, and government to initiate and finance programs for the small businessman, especially the black and brown businessman.

Until steps are taken to correct these inequities—either within a coalition or without it—frustrations will continue to build up, and the slightest provocative incident can lead to the kind of destructive violence we have witnessed in many cities all across the country. There are those who say that such revolt serves no useful purpose and that it cannot be condoned for any reason. Undoubtedly, such acts have contributed to the political "backlash" we have experienced in recent elections. But to deplore the revolts and yet to do nothing about the conditions that lead to frustration and end in violence is useless.

There is no time to talk about half-measures, no time to prosecute wars, no time to lash back at the angry poor, no time to moralize about unreachable utopias. Our collective wisdom must now be shaped into specific weapons of change. It is in this spirit—a spirit of crisis and a spirit of fragile hope—that we seek a political coalition to fight racism with the weapons of quality education, decent housing, meaningful employment, and political power. An alert, independent, and aggressive "third force," strengthened by the liberal arm of organized labor and other progressive groups, may be an important force in determining the political future of our black and brown community. A growing "third force" vote could bring changes of far-reaching importance throughout the nation. The success of such a political coalition could mean a significant change in Mexican-American and Afro-American power in this country.

There has been a healing of the rift between the Afro-American and the Mexican-American communities. Most of us recognize this. The division came about because these two minority groups had suffered too much discrimination, too much deprivation by the power structure. Neither Mexican-Americans nor Afro-Americans have been treated as full-fledged citizens in this country. Both Afro-Americans and Mexican-Americans want the rights and privileges long denied them, but they are not willing to lose their own identities. The answer to the question of how to gain these rights and privileges must come from those of us who face this question every day.

That Afro-Americans and Mexican-Americans are joining in their struggle against conditions which they can no longer tolerate is shown by some recent trends. During the past eighteen months, leaders of the two minorities have met, talked, planned, and acted. Here are the events pointing to a political coalition that may lead to success:

1. The peace pact between Tijerina and black power groups.

2. The appearance of Bert Corona, president of MAPA (Mexican-American Political Association) at the National Conference of Black Elected Officials in Chicago in 1967.

3. My appearance at the MAPA board meeting in San Diego in 1967 and the subsequent motion to form a coalition between blacks and browns.

4. The joint meeting of the California Conference of Black Elected Officials and the Legislative Conference of Spanish-Speaking Organizations in Sacramento in February, 1968.

5. The joint press conference of Tijerina, Corona, and Dymally.

6. The working relationship between La Raza groups and the Black Congress in Los Angeles.

7. The joint leadership of blacks and browns during the Poor People's March on Sacramento and on Washington, D.C., in 1968.

These are the visible signs of an active coalition, or at least the beginnings of one. Whether the vast majorities of the two communities will join in strong political action remains to be seen.

Amazingly enough, it is the black leadership, although successful in many ways in political processes, which has failed to create a strong state-wide political arm embracing all the black communities. The Mexican-American community has MAPA, which is getting politically stronger, especially in Los Angeles (witness Dr. Julian Nava's election), but the Negro Political Action Association is dead.

I think there are at least three reasons why the two minorities together have not proved to be stronger as a political force, even though each has made some modified gains separately. First, both the Mexican-Americans and the Afro-Americans tend to be too involved in emotional politics, and not enough involved in power politics. Second, the leaders of both groups are too anxious to serve the white master without questioning his motives. Third, neither group is willing to criticize its white liberal friends when they are practicing what are really forms of racism. These truths should be self-evident. For too long, we have been regarded as blocs of votes, large enough to swing elections but too unsophisticiated to demand our rights. If we are to be an effective political force, we must weld our communities into action blocs, not only voting blocs.

To begin a successful program of coalition, we should start with an organization and a paid staff. We should demand a greater voice in both political parties, and we should refuse to participate unless we have an equal voice in the decision-making of both the Democratic and Republican parties. These, too, should be self-evident truths.

One of the most perceptive analyses of the crisis situation was made recently by James Farmer, who urged reformers to recognize "the fierce desire of the young ghetto and *barrio* dweller to control his community and determine his destiny. Instead of viewing the black and brown youth as raw material to be bleached in a flock of white Americanism . . . we must begin to see him as a whole man, resentful and desperate for pride and identity, anxious to better his lot, but in jobs that bear his individual stamp and in industries where he commands power and a measure of ownership."

What is sought is liberation for America's domestic colonies —economic development with emphasis on self-help and self-determination. When one goes beyond the rhetoric of angry men, it would seem to mean, essentially, that black and brown people should control those institutions serving primarily their own people, that they should possess control over all institutions serving their population, and that they should have a fair share of participation in the economic and political forces which control the nation generally.

The late Robert F. Kennedy reminded us: "It is a revolutionary world we live in; and this generation, at home and around the world has had thrust upon it a greater burden of responsibility than any generation that has ever lived." He went on to say, "The future does not belong to those who are content with today, apathetic toward common problems and their fellow man alike, timid and fearful in the face of new ideas and bold projects. Rather, it will belong to those who can blend vision, reason, and courage in a personal commitment to the ideals and great enterprises of American society."

This is worth fighting for. This should be the aim of the new coalition.

Selected Questions and Answers

Q. "Was there, first of all, a black and Mexican-American political coalition in the march to Washington in 1968, and, if your answer is 'yes,' what happened?"

A. "So far, the coalition hasn't been structured. There have been loose associations and negotiations. The Spanish-speaking leadership did take part in the Poor People's March, and they spoke with Dr. King and Dr. Abernathy, but we have not been able to structure anything. I hope that with a possible grant we will be able to begin structuring some kind of coalition. It's difficult, in professional, pragmatic organizing, to put anything together without a staff."

Q. "Wasn't there a break between the Mexican-Americans and the black community?"

A. "No, that happens all the time. There are breaks between the whites, too, you know. We all have differences. The Mexican-American wants to have his own identity, and could, and should. I know that the black middle class has been indifferent to the Mexican-American's farm problems. There is no question about that. Also, the old-line Mexican-Americans did not want to identify themselves with the civil rights movement. I think that is changing now. The radical groups of young people don't want to be white, as the old-line Mexican-Americans wanted to be. They just want to be what they are. I think we are beginning to notice some changes. I am not too optimistic about the black and brown middle classes at this time, however."

Q. "You said that the political system is against revolution. Do you have any optimism that changes will come about? Do you think that the 'third force' will work in time?"

A. "Well, I think that the Peace and Freedom Party is an encouraging development. The difficulty with the Peace and Freedom Party is that a pragmatic politician must depend on Democratic votes to be elected, and so it is difficult for me to structurally associate myself with it. Until the structure of the party is really developed within my district, some joker would probably beat me if I tried to run on the Peace and Freedom Party ticket. So I am stuck, and that is why I think that a new 'third force' made up of the white student, the Mexican-American, the Afro-American, and what's left of the liberal labor movement could be put together in a more broadly-based coalition with some hope of success. This general grouping of factions has been called the 'New Politics.' "

Q. "Why is it that we cannot develop a sense of purpose in the minority groups in terms of voting power?"

A. "Political parties are not relevant to minorities. White people always say to me, 'Why don't Negroes register and vote?' But what change has registering to vote brought about on the American scene? When you look at it pessimistically, you know."

Q. "Local politics has produced change."

A. "Yes, sometimes, some changes. Even when we have one working on the inside and one on the outside, it still doesn't make a whole lot of change. Do you see any change in the Senate since I have been there?

"A formal complaint was filed against a committee chairman who 'fast-gavelled' a bill, and that chairman was me. 'Fast-gavelling' happens every day. The three guys on the committee say 'No,' and the committee chairman says, 'The bill is out.' But I did it, and they filed a complaint and almost broke the tradition of the Senate. The only way I could fight it was to say, 'Look, if you do it against me, all you cats are going to be subjected to complaints,' and then they withdrew it.

"One of the things I do now, because of the lack of visibility of the black elected officials in the legislature, is to move out into the community and do some things that have visibility, so that a brother can say, 'Dymally is doing this over here.'

"Keep in mind that the average black from the South, or the average Mexican-American from the Southwest, has not participated in the body politic for over a century. He comes to California, and all of a sudden a white person wants him to register. To vote for what? He has been denied that right for so long that it has no relevance to him. He has never been part of the political process, and one must understand that. So I don't get all shook up about registration drives anymore."

Q. "Could you speak a bit on the role of the so-called 'white liberal'?"

A. "That's my favorite subject. In the first place, the white liberal doesn't want to be a follower; he wants to lead. He doesn't want to follow black people on black issues; he wants to lead them. They have got to learn to follow, and they have got to stop acting as the spokesmen for minority communities.

"A good example: As you know, I was one of the strong supporters of Robert Kennedy in 1968. Black people and Mexican-American people had nothing to do with the setting up of that campaign. They didn't select their delegates. I was selected without my knowledge, consent, or permission. Some Democrat from a Republican district selected me because he thought I was convenient or something. This is the truth—he selected me, and I had nothing to do with it. As greatly as the black and Mexican-American voters were committed to Kennedy, they had nothing to do with the structure of his campaign, and that is the tragedy of American politics. There we sat, helpless. We made no decisions, not even about our constituents or people—no power was shared. As a matter of fact, they were mad at me because I questioned them publicly about running a racist campaign. And what was so bad about it was that there were black and brown people who were willing to abide by this tokenism.

"The white liberal doesn't want to go back to his own community. He wants to work in the black community and the Mexican-American community. But he's got to change things in his own community; he's got to tell the man that that's not the way it ought to be. When he goes down to Watts, he ought to check it out with the one who represents that district. He proceeds to make policy and to have us follow it. That is not the way.

"And the universities should know that black people in Watts and Mexican-American people in East Los Angeles are paying taxes, just for upper middle-class people to go to college. And so the crusade has to be done in their community, because I think we know how to talk to the brothers and sisters."

A Chicano Response

Samuel Soto Ortega

Since my name does not appear on the lecture program, perhaps this should be the first thing to be explained. A few weeks ago, a copy of today's program, "Ethnic Conflict in California History" came across my desk. Upon reviewing its contents, I immediately became concerned, and you might even say perturbed, when I noticed the absence of Spanish-surname speakers. I went through a series of telephone calls until I made contact with Mr. Wollenberg, who invited me to respond to Senator Dymally on the question of the black and brown coalition.

However, I would first like to comment on some of the observations I have made as a member of the audience during the past two days. I feel I must make these comments before the Senator and I can share the podium. I have been here two days, and I am sure that the Senator, who has been with us only part of today, will understand.

Para el beneficio de la audencia, por si acaso hay aquí unas personas que crean que yo soy un Tío Tomas, les quiero dar a saber que mi primera idioma fue español y la aprendí de me madre.

As I mentioned earlier, I did not come here with a prepared speech, but I did come with a conviction that somehow we can help each other to understand the problems of the Mexican-American. I can best impart my feelings and convictions by commenting on the various presentations that were made. I might add, since there is no bibliography on me, that I am not a doctor as have been most of the speakers before you, but, on the other hand, I do have some credentials that qualify me for the comments I will be making.

I believe that the speakers for these past two days have been —and I stand to be corrected if I am wrong—historians and research people. Well, I'm not an historian or a research person, but I can tell you how a Mexican-American feels about the findings of these historians and research people. My comments are made to point out to you that many of the conditions and much of the mentality that existed early in the history of this country still exist in present-day America.

First, we learn quite vividly that this country has an exceptionally long history of outright racial discrimination against black people, Mexicans, Chinese, Japanese, and other sizeable ethnic groups. Second, ours has been an ambitious and aggressive country that has taken land from other nations by the use of subversion, force, or whatever means were deemed necessary and appropriate to satisfy the Anglo's quest for conquest and expansion.

Dr. Borah, who spoke of the Spanish conquest, emphasized that the Indian would always be a part of the pyramid during the period of colonization. It was the intention of the Spanish, who in fact represented a European mentality, that the Indian would constitute the base of the pyramid, with little or no opportunity for upward mobility along social and economic lines. So, now, I have a question: Isn't it true that the Indian of that time, who has now become the Mexican-American, is still at the bottom of the pyramid? Dr. Cook stated that, after the American conquest of 1846, no effort was made to use these existing human resources to help develop the country. Instead, the country went to other nations to find its needed human resources and even went so far as to import slaves, which only served to augment the plight of the lower class. But on the question of not using a country's human resources, doesn't this still happen today? One of the richest human resources this country has is its black people and brown people. In spite of this wealth, even today we are sending representatives to African countries and to Latin America who cannot speak the languages and who cannot even relate to the people of those countries. Wouldn't it be more prestigious for this country to send envoys who were truly bilingual and bicultural? It seems to me that it is highly desirable that we have diplomats who have the ability to participate readily in two cultures as well as the ability to speak in two languages. Although we have this wealth among us, we are doing very little to develop its unique potential.

Dr. Borah said something else. He commented that between forced labor and slave labor there is very little difference. On this question I submit to you that the Mexican field laborers brought to the United States under the Bracero Program from the 1940's through 1965 were the same as slaves. The effects of this wholesale importation of captive labor very decidedly contributed to the image of the Anglo that Mexican-Americans are nothing but second-class citizens. Many of you will recall the famous remark of Senator George Murphy, who said that the Mexican bracero is particularly suited for farm work because he is built short to the ground. Now, some people have said, "Well, that's not what he really meant." I agree that's not what he really meant. My argument is that if a man in this country can reach the point where he can make such low statements as that without thinking of the consequences, then our fight must be to overcome such closed-minded mentality, such Anglo superiority. Just because a man is shorter in stature and darker of skin doesn't make him any less of a man.

Mr. Wollenberg spoke of the problems of the Mexican-American farm workers, and I must commend him for he is very knowledgeable about Mexican-American society. As a Mexican-American, I would like to comment briefly on the feelings I have about how the Mexican-American society differs from the Anglo. I was employed by the State of California for over five years, and during that period I worked for various agencies in different cities. When I was dealing with the Anglo community, if I mentioned that I was a state employee, they immediately wanted to know what my title was and how much money I made per month. On the other hand, when I touched bases with the Mexican-American community, they asked me my full name and where I came from. What I am trying to point out here is the difference in values and orders of importance between these two societies. The Anglo's most immediate concern is power and influence. The Mexican-American is more concerned with humanistic values of kinship and community linkage.

Dr. Rischin talked of the alternatives available to a large ethnic group such as the Mexican-Americans; they were (1) coexistence, (2) assimilation, and (3) synthesis. I say we can have co-existence, for we are a large ethnic group that is approximating three million alone in California and some eleven million throughout the country. You will recall that some of the other speakers discussed the tremendous attrition rate among minority groups. However, the reverse is true of the Mexican-American community. Not only does our segment of the population grow faster than any other minority group in America, but we must also recognize that the conditions which were conducive to attrition and accelerated it in the past are no longer as strong or prevalent as they were before.

But a desire for co-existence in itself is not going to bring about co-existence. After the Emancipation Proclamation, the United States established banks and colleges for black Americans. These institutions have produced many outstanding black Americans who have contributed and will continue to contribute to the wealth of America. Throughout my remarks, I keep emphasizing that the Mexican-American is proud as hell, but when we get down to dealing with the facts of life, we have to tell it like it is. Everyone needs a push or a helping hand, and the Mexican-American needs it too. If we review American history, we will find that this country, particularly in the West, has always found some minority to exploit—Chinese, Japanese, Filipino, Hindu, Negro, or Indian. It seems that there has always been room for each of these ethnic groups to go "somewhere." There is no room for the Mexican-American to move anywhere, and he certainly will not move into obscurity. You are going to have to deal with him; and you are going to have to understand him.

We should at this point make the clear distinction that Americans of Mexican descent have never actually, in the tradi-

tional sense, immigrated to the United States. They have simply
migrated only a few hundred miles from the northern border of
Mexico, and many more are just plain third- and fourth-generation Americans of pure Mexican heritage whose great-grand-
fathers were once proud landowners of the Southwest. It is not
uncommon for a family whose name may be Sanchez to leave
Hermosillo, Sonora, move to Los Angeles, California, and live
on Sepulveda Boulevard next to the Gomez family. This is exactly
what has happened over the past one hundred years, families
moving and relocating and yet remaining within the same community and style of living.

On the question of co-existence and the kind of support that
goes with co-existence, we shall call on some very strong Americans with the perception and courage to make decisions that will
bring about profound changes. In 1965, the Secretary of Labor,
Willard Wirtz, said that the Bracero Program was illegal and
immoral, and that it was going to be phased out. Mexican-
Americans had been relentlessly arguing this point for fifteen
years; one man, once convinced of the morality of the issue, did
it all with one stroke of the pen. President Johnson, who was
from Texas and who had recognized the problem, through executive order established the Inter-Agency Committee on Mexican-
American Affairs. Its Commissioner, Vicente Ximenez, who
has the power to cut through bureaucratic red tape at the top
levels of the federal government, has done a tremendous job.
Last year the Inter-Agency Committee held hearings in El Paso,
Texas, that brought together many Mexican-American leaders
to meet for two days with members of the President's Cabinet.
The Inter-Agency Committee now annually publishes a book
listing all Spanish-surname college graduates. This was done to
deal with the old problem of government, institutions, and employers saying, "We cannot find qualified Mexican-Americans."

One of the things we as Americans of Mexican descent
would like to see is more recognition in our educational system
of the contributions of Mexicans. Perhaps in present California
our contributions have not been so numerous, but the entire his-

tory of the Southwest is studded with an array of contributions from many Mexicans, contributions which helped to make this the richest and most powerful country in the world. Little has been told of the outstanding war record of Mexican-Americans. During World War II, eighteen Mexican-Americans were awarded the nation's highest military honor, the Congressional Medal of Honor. During Korea and Viet Nam, no turncoats by the names of Garcia, Martinez, or Rodriquez were recorded. We must look to the near future for more Mexican-Americans to make outstanding contributions in areas outside the military. Americans of Mexican descent have the same creativeness, desire, and intellect as their brothers who reside in Mexico and who prepared the 1968 World Olympics, an undertaking reputed to be a creation equal to the other wonders of the world.

But while we may mention our desire to contribute to our country, the United States, we must also accept the fact that we have some enormous obstacles to overcome. If I sound bitter, as I speak to you, it is because I am.

I am bitter because it hurts me to know there are annually some 25,000 migrant farm workers and their families who leave the Rio Grande Valley of Texas and travel through California, Oregon, Washington, Arizona, and back to Texas without receiving a decent education for their children. It hurts me to have come from a family of thirteen and to know I'm the only one who finished high school and had the good fortune of going on to college.

I am bitter because it hurts me to know that of San Quentin's inmates, 700 or 30 per cent are Mexican-Americans, and that over 70 per cent of them are there because of narcotics violations.

If I sound bitter, it is because I have appeared before superintendents of schools and have found out for myself that Mexican kids, unable to pass middle-class-oriented Anglo tests, are placed in classes for the mentally retarded.

If I sound bitter, it is because I have appeared before legislatures to seek their support for establishing a state multi-service center in San Francisco's Mission District similar to the one in the Fillmore District for the black community of San Francisco —and they have failed us.

If I sound bitter, it is because when I worked as a group supervisor at Preston School of Industry (a California Youth Authority camp), I was one of two Mexican-Americans trying to deal with young inmates of whom over 20 per cent were Mexican-American.

These barriers to first-class citizenship must be overcome through the combined efforts of the dominant society and the Mexican-American community. And if we are to overcome these barriers, then programs that emphasize Mexican-American leadership must be developed in each community where there is a sizeable Mexican-American population. In my opinion, the Mexican-American will never attain first-class citizenship in this country until he develops or is helped to develop his own leadership. He must share proportionately in political, economic, and social power. To deny this as a prerequisite is to admit that the dominant society is willing to open a few doors, but at the same time is adamant on having control of the decision-making.

Since World War II, the Mexican-American has been making significant gains to achieve a better way of life. This movement was underway before World War II, but it has now gained much more momentum and forcefulness. In 1966, I attended a Mexican-American Political Association endorsing convention in Fresno, where the unionization efforts of César Chavez were being discussed. A group of older farm workers involved in the *huelga* said, "We have talked about unionization and the deplorable working conditions of farm workers since the 1930's, but always before we talked about them while sitting along the banks of rivers, and now we speak publicly and through a microphone and at a convention of Mexican-Americans with press coverage and where Anglo politicians come to get our vote."

There is a great awakening in the Mexican-American community to the necessity of doing things for themselves. Throughout the years, many outstanding Mexican-American leaders have contributed to this movement, but the big push is coming from our Mexican-American youth. While many of us have been talking about the problems, the youth are pressing for solutions. They say they are Chicanos because they want it to be known that there will be no more hanky-panky behind the scenes, no more wheeling and dealing. They want solutions now, and they are prepared to make whatever demands are necessary in order to make the social issues of America today relevant to the Mexican-American—there is no middle-ground!

Because of this awakening, we already see many changes taking place. But it is only a start. The movement will get bigger and bigger. This is not to say that we have never had strong Mexican-American leadership in our own community—we have —but for too long we maintained an attitude of total respect and courtesy toward the Anglo. After years of ignorance, we see that Anglo educational, political, and social systems have been highly discriminatory and have failed miserably to help us become first-class citizens. The changes that we seek will be brought about through the efforts of strong state-wide organizations such as MAPA, Quinto Sol, MAYA, CSO, the G.I. Forum, the Brown Berets, NAFWA, UMAS, and AMAE, to mention only a few. There are many others which are local in nature but which are equally committed to making changes for the betterment of the Mexican-American community and in the interest of a well-rounded, well-functioning American society representative of all Americans—a society that will include bilingual, bicultural first-class citizens.

You must excuse me for having taken quite a bit of time to comment on my observations of these past two days. I mentioned earlier that my original purpose for being here this afternoon was to respond to Senator Dymally on the question of the black and brown coalition. At this point in the development of the black and brown people's movement to achieve status, the question cannot be answered with any great degree of precision. The proposition for a "coalition," as presented by Senator Dymally at the March, 1968, Second Annual Spanish-Speaking Issues

Conference in Sacramento, has gone back to the various Mexican-American organizations for approval. We all recognize the
need for a coalition, but it will take a great deal of discussion to
decide how this coalition should be set up. The move for a coalition on the part of the Mexican-American community is being
spearheaded by MAPA. At the MAPA meetings I have attended, everyone has agreed on the principle in general, but
there remain many questions about what strategy should be
employed.

In my opinion, to some extent there already exists between
us a sort of "unannounced coalition," but what Senator Dymally
speaks of is perhaps an officially-sanctioned coalition of solidarity and unity directed toward the accomplishment of specific
objectives. For this effort the Senator must be commended. To
say the least, I was very much impressed when I learned that he
was accompanied to the Spanish-Speaking Issues Conference by
at least fifteen or twenty outstanding black community leaders.
However, on the question of a coalition, I can only offer my opinion because I do not represent the proponents of this move. Personally, I feel that the time is right to be talking about a coalition, but that the firming-up of such a move will require quite a
bit more time and work. First, in the political arena, at the
national and state levels, there are very few Mexican-American
legislators. On the other hand, the Negro has always had some
representation and is now making more inroads. At the community and municipal levels, neither of the two groups has any
substantial representation. This is particularly true in California.
Second, War on Poverty money made available to many communities through the Office of Economic Opportunity has tended
to split the two communities rather than unite them. As a consequence, there is a growing distrust on the part of Mexican-
Americans about the significance of a coalition, since in the past
it has been a matter of record that Mexican-Americans have
shared disproportionately in the federal dollar as compared to the
black community. This situation must be remedied, and positive
steps must be taken to bring the two communities together on

these two issues. Another point to consider is the lack of concern the Anglo has had for the problems of the Mexican-American. This has not been the case for the black community. Many foundations, and especially those of the Jewish community, have provided them a great deal of moral and monetary assistance. In spite of these differences, however, a coalition is totally within the realm of possibility. But it seems to me that it will be incumbent upon the black community to demonstrate that they are willing to share and share alike in financial assistance and in economic and political power.

I find it difficult to find an appropriate ending for my remarks this afternoon. It would have been much easier for me to have used the time alloted to provide you with just another lecture in a series of lectures. Rather than do that, I chose to comment and to respond to the presentation already provided you. I am hopeful that I have added another dimension to your thinking. My point of view has been very much Mexican-American. Incidentally, I am somewhat amused that each time I asked the other speakers, "What is, or who is the Mexican-American?" the historians and research people would freeze on the question—after all, we are part of history! Fifty years from now they will do a beautiful job of research on us and they will provide you with some pat answers on the problems of today. Personally, I don't want to be researched any more; I want to be confronted. I don't want to be asked whether I am a Mexican-American or not. I want them to know what it is to be an American of Mexican descent.

Notes and Sources

Notes and Sources

Chapter I: "The California Mission" by Woodrow W. Borah

Suggested Readings

Bannon, John, ed. *Bolton and the Spanish Borderlands.* Norman: University of Oklahoma Press, 1964.

Bolton, Herbert E. *Rim of Christendom, a Biography of Eusebio Francisco Kino.* New York: Macmillan, 1936.

Cook, Sherburne F. *The Conflict Between the California Indian and White Civilization.* Berkeley, University of California Press, 1943.

Geiger, Maynard, J. *The Life and Times of Fray Junipero Serra.* Washington, D. C.: Academy of American Franciscan History, 1959.

Mission Santa Barbara. Santa Barbara: Franciscan Fathers, 1965.

Priestly, Herbert I. *José de Gálvez, Visitador General of New Spain.* Berkeley: University of California Press, 1916.

Chapter II: "The California Indian and Anglo-American Culture" by Sherburne F. Cook

References

1. General J. E. Wool, Benicia, September 15, 1855. United States National Archive, Office of Indian Affairs, Record Group 75, "Letters Received, California, 1856," Document H 22.

2. T. J. Henley, San Francisco, December 4, 1858. United States National Archive, Office of Indian Affairs, Record Group 75, "Letters Received, California, 1858," Document H 1335. See also F. F. Latta, Article No. 3, Livingstone (California) *Chronicle,* July 29, 1937, pp. 10–11.

3. D. N. Cooley, Tule River Farm, August 17, 1866, *Annual Report of the Commissioner of Indian Affairs* (Washington, D. C.: Office of Indian Affairs), p. 98, Document 19.
4. *Report of the Commissioner of Indian Affairs* (Washington, D. C.: Office of Indian Affairs, 1873), pp. 342–344.
5. C. Hart Merriam, "The Indian Population of California," *American Anthropologist* 7 (1905): 594–606.
6. W. W. Robinson, *The Indians of California, Story of the Liquidation of a People* (Los Angeles: Dawson, 1952), 43 pp.
7. "Correspondence from Ukiah," Sacramento (California) *Union,* August 19, 1865.
8. G. Bailey, Washington, October 2, 1858. United States National Archive, Office of Indian Affairs, Record Group 75, "Letters Received, California, 1858," Document B 611.

Chapter III: "Continuities and Discontinuities in Spanish-Speaking California" by Moses Rischin

References
1. For a more extended and elaborately documented critique of Western historiography, see Moses Rischin, "Beyond the Great Divide: Immigration and the Last Frontier," *The Journal of American History* 55 (June 1968): 42–53.
2. Earl Pomeroy, *The Pacific Slope: A History of California, Oregon, Washington, Idaho, Utah, and Nevada* (New York: Knopf, 1965), p. vi.
3. See Carey McWilliams, *Brothers Under the Skin,* rev. ed. (Boston: Little, Brown, 1951).
4. Rowland Berthoff, "The Social Order of the Anthracite Region, 1825–1902," *Pennsylvania Magazine of History and Biography* 89 (July 1965): 261–262.
5. See John Hicks, "California in History," *California Historical Society Quarterly* 24 (March 1945): 7–16.
6. See James Bryce, *The American Commonwealth* (New York: Macmillan, 1889).
7. See Henry George, *Progress and Poverty* (San Francisco: W. H. Hinton, 1879).
8. See Josiah Royce, *California From the Conquest in 1846 to the*

Second Vigilance Committee in San Francisco (New York: Houghton Mifflin, 1886).

9. Frank Soulé et al., *The Annals of San Francisco* ... (New York: D. Appleton & Co., 1855), p. 464–465.
10. Pomeroy, *op. cit.,* pp. 262–292.
11. John Francis Bannon, ed., *Bolton and the Spanish Borderlands* (Norman: University of Oklahoma Press, 1964), pp. 4, 9.
12. Nellie Sanchez, *Spanish Arcadia* (San Francisco: Powell, 1929), p. 378.
13. John Hawgood, *California as a Factor in World History During the Last Hundred Years* (Nottingham: University of Nottingham, 1948), p. 1.
14. John Higham et al., *History* (Englewood Cliffs, N. J.: Prentice-Hall, 1965), p. 41.
15. Leonard Pitt, *The Decline of the Californios: A Social History of the Spanish-Speaking Californians* (Berkeley: University of California Press, 1966).
16. See Cecil Robinson, *With the Ears of Strangers: The Mexican in American Literature* (Tucson: University of Arizona Press, 1963); Arthur J. Rubel, *Across the Tracks: Mexican-Americans in a Texas City* (Austin: University of Texas Press, 1966); John Tebbel, "Newest TV Boom: Spanish-Language Stations," *Saturday Review,* June 8, 1968, pp. 68–71.

Chapter IV: "Strangers in the Cities: The Chinese on the Urban Frontier" by Stanford M. Lyman

References

1. Georg Simmel, "The Stranger," *The Sociology of Georg Simmel,* translated and edited by Kurt Wolff (Glencoe: The Free Press, 1950), p. 402.
2. See Paul C. P. Siu, "The Sojourner," *American Journal of Sociology* 8 (July 1952): 32–44.
3. Cf. Harold Isaacs, *Images of Asia: American Views of China and India* (New York: Capricorn, 1962), pp. 63–238.
4. See Arthur O. Lovejoy, "The Chinese Origin of a Romanticism," *Essays in the History of Ideas* (New York: Capricorn, 1960), pp. 99–135.

5. Foster Rhea Dulles, *China and America: The Story of Their Relations Since 1784* (Princeton: Princeton University Press, 1946), pp. 6–7.
6. George H. Danton, *The Culture Contacts of the United States and China: The Earliest Sino-American Culture Contacts, 1784–1844* (New York: Columbia University Press, 1931), pp. 29, 33.
7. See Clay Lancaster, *The Japanese Influence in America* (New York: Walton H. Rawls, 1963), pp. 1–41.
8. Kenneth Scott Latourette, *The History of the Early Relations Between the United States and China, 1784–1844,* Transactions of the Connecticut Academy of Arts and Sciences 22 (August 1917): 16–17. Reprinted in 1964 by the Kraus Reprint Corporation, New York. See also Robert Glass Cleland, "Asiatic Trade and American Occupation of the Pacific Coast," *Annual Report of the American Historical Association for the Year 1914* (Washington, 1916) 1: 283–289. For Shaw's own account of his days in China, see Joseph Quincy, *The Journals of Major Samuel Shaw, the First American Consul at Canton, with a Life of the Author* (Taipei: Ch' eng-wen Publishing Co., 1968). Originally published in 1848.
9. See *China in the 16th Century: The Journals of Matthew Ricci, 1583–1610,* translated by Louis J. Gallagher, S. J. (New York: Random House, 1952), pp. 41–58. The "American farmer," J. Hector St. John de Crevecoeur, wrote in 1782 that "the American father thus ploughing with his child, and to feed his family, is inferior only to the emperor of China ploughing as an example to his kingdom." *Letters From An American Farmer* (New York: E. P. Dutton, 1957), p. 21. The 1765 catalogue of the private Union Library of Philadelphia contained among its titles *Chinese Tales,* a book so popular that the librarian had had to advertise for its return in 1764. Carl and Jessica Bridenbaugh, *Rebels and Gentlemen: Philadelphia in the Age of Franklin* (New York: Oxford Hesperides, 1962), p. 87.
10. See *Niles Register,* February 23, 1822, and June 18, 1835. Quoted in Danton, *op. cit.,* p. 11n. There was also a considerable respect for China's developments in agriculture and conveniences. Thus, the first volume of the *American Philosophical Society* wished that America "could be so fortunate as to introduce the industry of the Chinese, their arts of living, and improvements in husbandry... [so that] America might become in time as populous as China." And as late as 1840, *Hunt's Merchants' Magazine* wrote, "The

industry and ingenuity of the Chinese in all that relates to the conveniences of life are remarkable: the origin among them of several arts of comparatively recent date in Europe, is lost in the night of time." Quoted in Latourette, *op. cit.,* p. 124.

Respect for the Chinese government, originating in the sixteenth-century Jesuit praises of the Peking administration, died down after Lord Macartney vividly contrasted the old Chinese order with that imposed after 1644 by the Manchus. He wrote, "The government as it now stands is properly the tyranny of a handful of Tartars over more than three hundred millions of Chinese . . . . A series of two hundred years in the succession of eight or ten monarchs did not change the Mongol into a Hindu, nor has a century and a half made Ch'ien-lung a Chinese. He remains at this hour, in all his maxims of policy, as true a Tartar as any of his ancestors." *An Embassy to China: Being the Journal Kept by Lord Macartney During his Embassy to the Emperor Ch'ien Lung, 1793–1794,* edited by J. L. Cranmer-Byng (Hamden, Conn.: Archon, 1963), pp. 236–237. By the mid-nineteenth century, the Chinese emperor's ability to keep Anglo-American ministers from the capital and to bottle them up with local officialdom was a matter of keen consternation. See, for example, Laurence Oliphant, *Narrative of the Earl of Elgin's Mission to China and Japan in the Years 1857, '58, '59* (New York: Harper, 1860), pp. 276–281.

11. George I. Quimby, "Culture Contact on the Northwest Coast, 1785–1795," *American Anthropologist* 50 (April–June 1948): 247–255. See also Margaret Ormsby, *British Columbia: A History* (Vancouver: Macmillan, 1958), pp. 16–19.

12. Homer H. Dubs and Robert S. Smith, "Chinese in Mexico City in 1635," *Far Eastern Quarterly* 1 (August 1942): 387–389. See also William Lytle Schurz, *The Manila Galleon* (New York: E. P. Dutton, 1959), pp. 63–98.

13. For the Chinese in Pennsylvania, see R. L. Brunhouse, "Lascars in Pennsylvania: A Sidelight on the China Trade," *Pennsylvania History,* January, 1940, pp. 20–30. For the role of the Chinese in early New England, see Samuel Eliot Morison, *The Maritime History of Massachusetts, 1783–1860* (Boston: Houghton Mifflin, 1961), p. 354 et passim.

14. Dulles, *op. cit.,* p. 39.

15. Morison, *op. cit.,* p. 203.

16. Dulles, *loc. cit.;* Morison, *op. cit.,* pp. 240, 273.

17. Latourette, *op. cit.*, p. 123.
18. Danton, *op. cit.*, p. 102.
19. Charles Gold to George Danton. Reported in Danton, *op. cit.*, pp. 102–103.
20. For the life of Yung Wing see Yung Wing, *My Life in China and America* (New York: Henry Holt & Co., 1909); Lo Hsiang-lin, *Hong Kong and Western Cultures* (Honolulu: East West Center Press, 1964), pp. 86–156; Edmund H. Worthy, Jr., "Yung Wing in America," *Pacific Historical Review* 34 (August 1965): 265–288.
21. See Tyler Dennet, *Americans in Eastern Asia* (New York: Barnes and Noble, 1963), p. 545n for a personal report to this effect.
22. Y. C. Wang, *Chinese Intellectuals and the West, 1872–1949* (Chapel Hill: University of North Carolina Press, 1966), pp. 42–45. For the fate of the Chinese returnees, many of whom led distinguished lives in China, see Lo Hsiang-lin, *op. cit.*, pp. 125–144.
23. Richard H. Dillon, *The Hatchet Men: The Story of the Tong Wars in San Francisco's Chinatown* (New York: Coward-McCann, 1962), p. 30.
24. Howard M. Chapin, "The Chinese Junk Ke Ying at Providence," *Rhode Island Historical Society Collections* 27 (January 1934): 5–12.
25. For a popular account which, despite the authors' lack of social criticism, reveals the hostility directed against Chinese and the cruel pranks played upon them, see Lucius Beebe and Charles Clegg, "The Heathen Chinese," *The American West* (New York: E. P. Dutton, 1955), pp. 318–335. Mark Twain documented the numerous attacks on Chinese, attacks which took place nearly every day. See, for example, "Those Blasted Children," *New York Sunday Mercury*, March 27, 1864. Reprinted in Bernard Taper, ed., *Mark Twain's San Francisco* (New York: McGraw-Hill, 1963), pp. 27–33. Many of the songs of Gold Rush California derided the Chinese for his queue. See Richard A. Dwyer and Richard E. Lingenfelter, *The Songs of the Gold Rush* (Berkeley: University of California Press, 1964), pp. 112–113, 119, 121, et passim. The Chinese queue was also a stereotypical feature of humorous drama about the Chinese in the nineteenth century. See Stewart W. Hyde, "The Chinese Stereotype in American Melodrama," *California Historical Society Quarterly*, December, 1955, pp. 357–367.
26. B. S. Brooks, "History of the Legislation of the Supervisors of

the City of San Francisco Against the Chinese, Culminating in the Passage of the Present Ordinance Generally known as the 'Queue Cutting Ordinance'...," *The Invalidity of the Queue Ordinance of the City and County of San Francisco* (San Francisco: J. L. Rice and Co., 1879), Appendix: 15–43.

27.   Latourette, *op. cit.,* p. 123; Dillon, *op. cit.,* p. 30. The definitive work on the subject is Howard S. Levy, *Chinese Footbinding: The History of a Curious and Erotic Custom* (New York: Walton Rawls, 1966).

28.   Levy, *op. cit.,* pp. 95–99, 276–281.

29.   Thomas Taylor Meadows, *The Chinese and their Rebellions* (Stanford: Academic Reprints, n. d., originally published in 1856), pp. 34–50, 112–122; J. Thomson, *The Straits of Malacca, Indo-China, and China; or Ten Years' Travels, Adventures, and Residence Abroad* (New York: Harper, 1875), pp. 46–48.

30.   Ping-ti Ho, *Studies on the Population of China, 1368–1953* (Cambridge: Harvard University Press, 1959), pp. 101–280.

31.   Hosea Ballou Morse, *The Trade and Administration of the Chinese Empire* (Shanghai: Kelly and Walsh, 1908), pp. 175–351; John King Fairbank, *Trade and Diplomacy on the China Coast: The Opening of the Treaty Ports, 1842–1854,* 1 vol. ed. (Cambridge: Harvard University Press, 1964); W. C. Hunter, *The 'Fan Kwae' at Canton Before Treaty Days, 1825–1844* (Taipei: Ch'eng-wen Publishing Co., 1965); Victor Purcell, *China* (London: Ernest Benn, 1962), pp. 52–61; Edgar Holt, *The Opium Wars in China* (London: Putnam, 1964).

32.   "The Celestials at Home and Abroad," *Littell's Living Age* 430 (August 14, 1852): 294.

33.   *Loc. cit.*

34.   For a careful analysis of casualties during the Taiping Rebellion, see Ping-ti Ho, *op. cit.,* pp. 236–247, 275. The Taiping insurrection has been a continuous source of Sinological study. For some representative works, see Meadows, *op. cit.;* Vincent C. Y. Shih, *The Taiping Ideology: Its Sources, Interpretations and Influences* (Seattle: University of Washington Press, 1967); Franz Michael in collaboration with Chung-li Chang, *The Taiping Rebellion: History and Documents, Vol. I: History* (Seattle: University of Washington Press, 1966); Eugene Powers Boardman, *Christian Influence upon the Ideology of the Taiping Rebellion, 1851–1865* (Madison: University of Wisconsin Press, 1952); J. C. Cheng, *Chinese*

Sources for the Taiping Rebellion, 1850–1864 (Hong Kong: Hong Kong University Press, 1963); Lady Flavia Anderson, *The Rebel Emperor* (London: Victor Gollancz, 1958).

35. Oliphant, *op. cit.,* pp. 75–300; Meadows, *op. cit.,* pp. 75–492; Robert Fortune, *A Residence Among the Chinese: Inland, On the Coast, and at Sea; Being a Narrative of Scenes and Adventures During a Third Visit to China from 1853 to 1856 . . . With Suggestions on the Present War* (London: John Murray, 1857), pp. 1–22, 423–440; S. Wells Williams, *The Middle Kingdom: A Survey of the Geography, Government, Education, Social Life, Arts, Religion, etc., of the Chinese Empire and its Inhabitants . . . ,* 3rd ed., vol. 2 (New York: John Wiley, 1853), pp. 417–604. For the Hakka-Punti War, see Leon Comber, *Chinese Secret Societies in Malaya: A Survey of the Triad Society from 1800 to 1900* (Locust Valley, N. Y.: J. J. Augustin, 1959), pp. 28–29. For the American participation in the Taiping hostilities, see Robert S. Rantoul, *Frederick Townsend Ward: Organizer and First Commander of the 'Ever Victorious Army' in the Tai Ping Rebellion,* Historical Collections of the Essex Institute 44 (Salem: Essex Institute, 1908).

36. Arthur Waley, *The Opium War Through Chinese Eyes* (Stanford: Stanford University Press, 1968); Siang-Tseh Chiang, *The Nien Rebellion* (Seattle: University of Washington Press, 1954); *The Boxer Uprising: A History of the Boxer Trouble in China* (New York: Paragon, 1967); Victor Purcell,*The Boxer Uprising: A Background Study* (Cambridge: University Press, 1963).

37. "The Discovery of Gold in California," *Hutchings' California Magazine* 2 (November 1857): 194–202. Articles by John A. Sutter and James W. Marshall. Reprinted in John A. Hawgood, *America's Western Frontiers: The Exploration and Settlement of the Trans-Mississippi West* (New York: Knopf, 1967), pp. 189–198.

38. "Quite a large number of the Celestials have arrived among us of late, enticed hither by the golden romance which has filled the world. Scarcely a ship arrives here that does not bring an increase to this worthy integer of our population; and we hear, by China papers, and private advices from that empire, that the feeling is spreading all through the sea-board, and, as a consequence, nearly all the vessels that are up for this country are so for the prospect of passengers. A few Chinamen have returned, taking home with

them some thousands of dollars in California gold, and have thus given an impetus to the spirit of emigration from their fatherland which is not likely to abate for some years to come." *Daily Alta Californian,* May 12, 1851.

39. For circulars used in 1862, 1868, and 1870, see Hubert Howe Bancroft, *The New Pacific,* 3rd ed. (New York: The Bancroft Co., 1915), pp. 413–414.

40. A full discussion of all the ramifications of Chinese immigration is beyond the scope of this paper. For good accounts, see Pyau Ling, "Causes of Chinese Emigration," *Annals of the American Academy of Political and Social Science* 39 (January 1912): 74–82; Ta Chen, "Chinese Migrations, with Special Reference to Labor Conditions," *Bulletin of the United States Bureau of Labor Statistics,* No. 340 (Washington, D. C.: Government Printing Office, 1923); Wu Ching-ch'ao, "Chinese Immigration in the Pacific Area," *Chinese Social and Political Science Review* 12–13 (October 1928, January 1929, April 1929): 543–560, 50–76, 161–182; Tin-Yuke Char, "Legal Restrictions on Chinese in English-Speaking Countries of the Pacific," *Chinese Social and Political Science Review* 16 (January 4, 1933): 472–513.

41. See Warren B. Smith, *White Servitude in Colonial South Carolina* (Columbia: University of South Carolina Press, 1961); Carl Bridenbaugh, *Vexed and Troubled Englishmen, 1590–1642* (New York: Oxford University Press, 1968), pp. 210, 421–424; Oscar Handlin, *The Americans: A New History of the People of the United States* (Boston: Atlantic-Little, Brown, 1963), pp. 20–22.

42. See Theodore Saloutos, *They Remember America: The Story of the Repatriated Greek-Americans* (Berkeley: University of California Press, 1956), pp. 16–17; Oscar Handlin, *Boston's Immigrants, 1790–1880: A Study in Acculturation* (New York: Atheneum, 1968), pp. 70–71.

43. Persia Crawford Campbell, *Chinese Coolie Emigration to Countries within the British Empire* (London: King and Songs, 1923), pp. xvii–xix, 28–39, 150–151.

44. For a complete discussion, see Stanford M. Lyman, *The Structure of Chinese Society in Nineteenth Century America,* unpublished Ph.D. dissertation, University of California, Berkeley, 1961.

That the Chinese migrant to California was often the loser in an unprofitable venture is illustrated in this incident related by the distinguished historian Hosea Ballou Morse: "An incident which occurred to the author in 1893 throws some light on the usual result to a returned Chinese emigrant. At a railway station in Formosa he was addressed in fluent and correct English by the proprietor-cook of the station restaurant; and in answer to an expression of astonishment, the Chinese explained why he was there. He had returned from California with a fortune of $2000. He had first to disburse heavily to remain unmolested by the magistrate and his underlings; then he had to relieve the necessities of his aged father; then an uncle, who had fallen into business difficulties, must be rescued from impending bankruptcy; and then he found that he had only enough left to procure himself a wife, with a few dollars margin wherewith to establish himself in his present business, which at most would require $100 capital." *The International Relations of the Chinese Empire, Volume II: The Period of Submission, 1861–1893* (Taipei: Book World Co., n. d., originally published in 1910), p. 166n.

45.   For the early maltreatment of Chinese by American sea captains, see the account of the infamous *"Robert Brown* incident" in Earl B. Swisher, *China's Management of the American Barbarians: A Study of Sino-American Relations, 1841–1861* (New Haven: Far Eastern, 1951), pp. 179–205. For the corruption of American officials at Canton, see the testimony of Thomas H. King in *Report of the Joint Special Committee to Investigate Chinese Immigration,* U. S. Congress, Senate, 44th Congress, 2nd Session, Report No. 689, February, 1877, p. 93; testimony of Governor F. F. Low and testimony of Charles Wolcott Brooks in "Chinese Immigration: Its Social, Moral, and Political Effects," *Report to the California State Senate of its Special Committee on Chinese Emigration,* Sacramento, 1878, pp. 70, 101–102. See also Charles Wolcott Brooks, "The Chinese Labor Problem," *Overland Monthly,* November, 1869, pp. 407–419.

46.   The whole incident may be pieced together from documents and articles which appeared at the time. For the Memphis convention, see the report of its Committee on Chinese Labor in John R. Commons et al., *A Documentary History of American Industrial Society* (Cleveland: A. H. Clark, 1910–1911), 9: 80–84. The whole scheme was debated in the South's most prominent journal. See William M. Burwell, "Science and the Mechanic Arts Against

Coolies," *De Bow's Review* 7 (July 1869): 557–571; A. P. Merrill, "Southern Labor," *ibid.,* pp. 586–592; William M. Burwell, "The Cooley-ite Controversy," *De Bow's Review* 7 (August 1869): 709–724; "Our Chamber of Commerce—The Chinese Labor Question," *ibid.,* pp. 669–701. For the character of Tye Kim Orr, see Edward Jenkins, *The Coolie—His Rights and Wrongs* (New York: Routledge and Sons, 1871), pp. 114–116. For the Chinese reaction, see the testimony of T. H. King in *Report of the Joint Special Committee, op. cit.,* p. 93. For Koopmanschap, see Gunther Barth, *Bitter Strength: A History of the Chinese in the United States, 1850–1870* (Cambridge: Harvard University Press, 1964), pp. 60, 117, 190–196. For a contemporary favorable account of Koopmanschap's Southern plan, see "The Chinese Again," *Hunt's Merchants' Magazine* 61 (September 1869): 214–217.

47. Chinese had appeared in Kansas in 1859. During the Reconstruction period, gangs of Chinese were employed in various kinds of work in several southern states. See Barth, *op. cit.,* pp. 187–198. For the Chinese in Mississippi, see Robert W. O'Brien, "Status of Chinese in the Mississippi Delta," *Social Forces* 19 (March 1941): 386–390.

48. See, for example, Barth, *op. cit.,* p. 189.

49. Patricia K. Ourada, "The Chinese in Colorado," *The Colorado Magazine* 29 (October 1952): 273–283.

50. James J. O'Meara, "The Chinese in Early Days," *Overland Monthly* 4 (May 1884): 477.

51. Mary R. Coolidge, *Chinese Immigration* (New York: Henry Holt, 1909), pp. 22–25.

52. Signs of racism and xenophobia had appeared earlier. The hostilities to Australians, Chileans, Mexicans, Peruvians, and Pacific Islanders and the early attempts to bar Negroes from the state have been attributed by one recent careful researcher to the "respectable" American white middle class settlers' desire for "order." See Leonard Pitt, "The Beginnings of Nativism in California," *Pacific Historical Review* 30 (February 1961): 23–38. For a recent analysis of the Negro question in the West, see Eugene H. Berwanger, *The Frontier Against Slavery: Western Anti-Negro Prejudice and the Slavery Extension Controversy* (Urbana: University of Illinois Press, 1967). For an excellent example of California gubernatorial policy directed against the Negroes, see "The First

Annual Message of the Governor of California," December 21, 1849, *California Senate Journal; First Session,* 1849–1850, pp. 30–41.

53. For descriptions of Chinese miners, see "Mining Life in California," *Harper's Weekly,* October 3, 1857, pp. 632–634; J. D. Borthwick, *Three Years in California* (Edinburgh and London: Blackwood, 1857), chapter 17.

54. See "Report of the Committee on Mines and Mining Interests," *Assembly Journal,* California State Legislature, 4th session, 1853, Appendix: 7–12; see also Coolidge, *op. cit.,* pp. 26–40.

55. See *People vs. Downer* 7 Cal. 169 (1857); *Lin Sing vs. Washburn* 20 Cal. 534 (1863); *In re Ah Fong* 3 Sawyer 144 (1874); *Chy Lung vs. Freeman* 92 U. S. 275 (1876). See also Elmer C. Sandmeyer, "California Anti-Chinese Legislation and the Federal Courts: A Study in Federal Relations," *Pacific Historical Review* 5 (September 1936): 189–211.

56. For the attack at Chinese Camp, see Theodore Hittel, *History of California* (San Francisco: N. J. Stone, 1897), 4: 102. The resolution against Chinese miners in Marysville will be found in the Marysville *Herald,* May 4, 1852.

57. *Sacramento Union,* May 2, 1852.

58. Charles Howard Shinn, *Mining Camps: A Study in American Frontier Government,* edited by Rodman Wilson Paul (New York: Harper Torchbooks, 1965), p. 246. Originally published in 1884.

59. *Ibid.,* p. 248.

60. *Ibid.,* p. 213.

61. *Sacramento Union,* December 29, 30, 1858; March 5–10, July 16, 25, 1859. Coolidge, *op. cit.,* p. 255n.

62. "By 1859 the white miners had abandoned a large part of the American River, the original home of river mining, to the Chinese, and by the close of 1863 the Asiatics had inherited the greater part of the river claims throughout the state. The fact that the whites no longer desired the claims for themselves is conclusive evidence of the declining profitability of this once great type of mining." Rodman W. Paul, *California Gold: The Beginning of Mining in the Far West* (Lincoln: University of Nebraska Press, 1947), p. 130. See also Rodman W. Paul, *Mining Frontiers of the Far West, 1848–1880* (New York: Holt, Rinehart & Winston, 1963), pp. 35–36.

63. "How We Get Gold in California," *Harper's New Monthly Maga-*

zine, April, 1860. Reprinted in Milo Milton Quaife, *Pictures of Gold Rush in California* (New York: Citadel, 1967), p. 197.

64. *Ibid.,* p. 199.
65. *Up and Down California in 1860–1864: The Journal of William H. Brewer,* edited by Francis P. Farquhar (Berkeley: University of California Press, 1966), pp. 329–330, 455, 481.
66. Helen Rocca Goss, "The Celestials," *Life and Death of a Quicksilver Mine* (Los Angeles: Historical Society of Southern California, 1958), pp. 63–86.
67. Rossiter W. Raymond, *Statistics of Mines and Mining in the States and Territories West of the Rocky Mountains* (Washington, D. C.: Government Printing Office, 1872), p. 4. Quoted in Paul, *California Gold, op. cit.,* p. 322.
68. Paul, *California Gold, op. cit.,* pp. 329–330.
69. Lynwood Carranco, "Chinese Expulsion from Humboldt County," *Pacific Historical Review* 30 (November 1961): 329–340.
70. Charlotte T. Miller, *Grapes, Queues, and Quicksilver,* unpublished manuscript in possession of the author.
71. Larry D. Quinn, " 'Chink Chink Chinaman': The Beginnings of Nativism in Montana," *Pacific Northwest Quarterly* 58 (April 1967): 82–89.
72. A circular recruiting labor in Hong Kong for Oregon in 1862 tells part of the story: "To the countrymen of Au Chan! There are laborers wanted in the land of Oregon, in the United States, in America. There is much inducement to go to this new country, as they have many great works there which are not in our own country. They will supply good houses and plenty of food. They will pay you $28 a month after your arrival, and treat you considerately when you arrive. There is no fear of slavery. All is nice. The ship is now going and will take all who can pay their passage. The money required is $54. Persons having property can have it sold for them by correspondents, or borrow money of me upon security. I cannot take security on your children or your wife. Come to me in Hongkong and I will take care for you until you start. The ship is substantial and convenient. (Signed) Au Chan." Quoted in Rhoda Hoff, *America's Immigrants: Adventures in Eyewitness History* (New York: Henry Z. Walck, 1967), pp. 74–75. For the rise and decline of Chinese miners in Oregon, see Paul, *Mining Frontiers, op. cit.,* p. 149.
73. *Ibid.,* pp. 143–144.

74. Rose Hum Lee, *The Chinese in the United States of America* (Hong Kong: Hong Kong University Press, 1960), pp. 189–190.

75. James M. Hulse, *The Nevada Adventure: A History* (Reno: University of Nevada Press, 1966), p. 79.

76. Dan DeQuille (pseudonym for William Wright), *History of the Big Bonanza: An Authentic Account of the Discovery, History, and Working of the World Renowned Comstock Silver Lode of Nevada* (San Francisco: Hartford Publishing Co., A. L. Bancroft & Co., 1876). The section on Chinatown is reprinted in Robert Kirsch and William S. Murphy, *West of the West: Witnesses to the California Experience, 1542–1906* (New York: E. P. Dutton, 1967), pp. 409–411.

77. *The Chinese Massacre at Rock Springs, Wyoming Territory, September 2, 1885* (Boston: Franklin Press, Rand Avery and Co., 1886). For a debate over whether the Chinese "deserved" to be the victims of a riotous lynch mob, see A. A. Sargent, "The Wyoming Anti-Chinese Riot," *Overland Monthly* 6 (November 1885): 507–512, and J., " 'The Wyoming Anti-Chinese Riot'—Another View," *Overland Monthly* 6 (December 1885): 573–576.

78. Pierre Lamoureux, "Les premieres annees de l'immigration chinoise au Canada," *Revue Canadienne de Geographie* 9 (January–March 1955): 9–28.

79. Ormsby, *op. cit.,* pp. 167, 281.

80. Ted C. Hinckley, "Prospectors, Profits, and Prejudice," *The American West* 2 (Spring 1965): 58–65.

81. *Tombstone Epitaph,* February 13, 1882. Quoted in Duane A. Smith, *Rocky Mountain Mining Camps: The Urban Frontier* (Bloomington: Indiana University Press, 1967), p. 31.

82. *Owyhee Avalanche,* June 23, 1866. Quoted in Smith, *op. cit.,* p. 32.

83. *Montanian,* March 27, 1873. Quoted in Larry Barsness, *Gold Camp: Alder Gulch and Virginia City, Montana* (New York: Hastings House, 1962), p. 239.

84. *Governor's Message, Delivered to the Two Houses of the Montana Legislative Assembly at Virginia City,* December 11, 1869 (Helena, 1869), p. 8. Quoted in Quinn, *op. cit.,* p. 83. Cf. "Special Message from the Governor of California to the Senate and Assembly of California in Relation to Asiatic Emigrations," *California Senate Journal; Third Session,* April 23, 1852.

85. Springfield *Republican,* June 7, 1870; Boston *Transcript,* June 13,

1870; Boston *Commonwealth,* June 25, 1870; Boston *Investigator,* July 6, 1870. See also Frederick Rudolph, "Chinamen in Yankeedom: Anti-Unionism in Massachusetts," *American Historical Review* 53 (October 1947): 1–29.

86. Albert Rhodes, "The Chinese at Beaver Falls," *Lippincott's Magazine* 19 (June 1877): 708–714.

87. Cincinnati *Enquirer,* January 8, April 11, June 24, 1870; Cleveland *Leader,* June 6, 1870; *Ohio State Journal,* November 3, 1873. Quoted in Carl Wittke, *We Who Built America* (New York: Prentice-Hall, 1948), pp. 460–461.

88. Samuel Gompers, *Seventy Years of Life and Labor: An Autobiography* (New York: E. P. Dutton, 1925), 1: 216–217, 304–305; 2: 162–169. For Gompers' racism, see Herbert Hill, "The Racial Practices of Organized Labor—the Age of Gompers and After," in Arthur Ross and Herbert Hill, eds., *Employment, Race, and Poverty: A Critical Study of the Disadvantaged Status of Negro Workers, from 1865 to 1965* (New York: Harcourt, Brace & World, 1967), pp. 365–402.

89. Selig Perlman, *The History of Trade Unionism in the United States* (New York: Augustus Kelley, 1950), p. 62.

90. See Stanford M. Lyman, "Contrasts in the Community Organization of Chinese and Japanese in North America," *Canadian Review of Sociology and Anthropology* 5 (May 1968): 51–67.

91. For the Chinese in agriculture, see Carey McWilliams, *Factories in the Fields: The Story of Migratory Farm Labor in California* (Boston: Little, Brown, 1939), pp. 66–80; Carey McWilliams, *Southern California Country: An Island on the Land* (New York: Duell, Sloan, and Pearce, 1946), pp. 84–95; Ping Chiu, *Chinese Labor in California, 1850–1880* (Madison: State Historical Society of Wisconsin, 1963), pp. 67–88.

92. Rose Hum Lee, "The Decline of Chinatowns in the United States," *American Journal of Sociology,* March, 1949, pp. 422–432.

93. For the Chinese in railroad work, see Alexander Sexton, "The Army of Canton in the High Sierra," *Pacific Historical Review* 35 (May 1966): 141–152. Chinese were employed in digging the tunnels for California's vineyards; many were killed in tunnel collapses. They also worked as pickers of grapes, strawberries, cotton, and other crops, and at a variety of other laboring and menial tasks. See A. W. Loomis, "How Our Chinamen Are Employed,"

Overland Monthly, March 1869, pp. 231–240; H. C. Bennett, "The Chinese in California, Their Numbers and Significance," *Sacramento Daily Union,* November 27, 1869, p. 8; Ping Chiu, *op. cit.,* pp. 40–128.

94. Testimony of the Hon. Frank M. Pixley, *Report of the Joint Special Committee, op. cit.,* p. 12.

95. See the table in Coolidge, *op. cit.,* p. 503.

96. The diaspora of Chinese since the sixteenth century has made Chinatown an ubiquitous phenomenon in countries of Asia, Africa, Europe, and Latin America. For some representative descriptions, see Shelland Bradley, "Calcutta's Chinatown," *Cornhill Magazine* 57 (September 1924): 277–285; Tsien-Tche-hao, "La vie sociale de Chinois a Madagascar," *Comparative Studies in Society and History* 3 (January 1961): 170–181; A. Dupouy, "Un camp de Chinois," *Reveue de Paris* 26 (November 1919): 146–162; P. Le Monnyer, "Les Chinois de Paris," *L'Illustration* 82 (November 1, 1924): 406–407; Christopher Driver, "The Tiger Balm Community," *The Guardian,* January 2, 1962; Ng Kwee Choo, *The Chinese in London* (London: Oxford University Press, 1968): Leonard Broom, "The Social Differentation of Jamaica," *American Sociological Review* 19 (April 1954): 115–124.

97. See Maurice Freedman, *Lineage Organization in Southeastern China* (London: The Athlone Press, 1958), and *Chinese Lineage and Society: Fukien and Kwangtung* (London: The Athlone Press, 1966).

98. "Whenever any persons having the same family name intermarry, the parties and the contractor of the marriage shall each receive 60 blows, and the marriage being null and void, the man and woman shall be separated, and the marriage-presents forfeited to the government." Sir George Thomas Staunton, *Tsa Tsing Leu Lee: Being the Fundamental Laws and a Selection from the Supplementary Statutes of the Penal Code of China* . . . (London, 1810), p. 114. Quoted in Freedman, *Lineage Organization, op. cit.,* p. 4n. Overseas this rule has been relaxed as more and more Chinese-Americans refuse to recognize an incest taboo that runs counter to that of the American kinship system. However, only a decade ago, one Chinese-American college student told me that his mother would be furious if she knew he was dating a girl with his own surname. Clan exogamy has been seen as one of the principal reasons

for the decline of the small (i.e., four-clan) Chinatowns in the United States. Marriageable men migrate to the larger urban Chinese communities to have a greater choice in mate selection. See Rose Hum Lee, "The Decline of Chinatowns," *op. cit.*

99. San Francisco Chinese Chamber of Commerce, *San Francisco's Chinatown, History, Function, and Importance of Social Organization* (San Francisco, 1953), pp. 2–4. Space does not permit a complex discussion of overseas clans. See Lyman, *The Structure of Chinese Society, op. cit.*, pp. 164–178, and William Willmott, "Chinese Clan Associations in Vancouver," *Man* 64 (March–April 1964): 33–37.

100. See Chinese Chamber of Commerce, *op. cit.*, p. 3. See also the discussion in Rose Hum Lee, *The Chinese in the United States of America, op. cit.*, pp. 136–137, 164–165, 264.

101. See Calvin Lee, *Chinatown, U. S. A.: A History and Guide* (Garden City: Doubleday, 1965), pp. 31–34. For the nature of the intra-clan disputes and disharmony, see Milton L. Barnett, "Kinship as a Factor Affecting Cantonese Economic Adjustment in the United States," *Human Organization* 19 (Spring 1960): 40–46.

102. The definitive work on the subject is Ping-ti Ho, *Chung-kuo hui-kuan shih-lueh* [An historical survey of Landsmannschaften in China] (Taipei: Student Publishing Co., 1966). For brief accounts, see Ping-ti Ho, "Salient Aspects of China's Heritage," in Ping-ti Ho and Tang Tsou, eds., *China in Crisis: China's Heritage and the Communist Political System* (Chicago: University of Chicago Press, 1968), vol. 1, book 1, pp. 34–35; and Francis L. K. Hsu, "Chinese Kinship and Chinese Behavior," *ibid.*, vol. 1, book 2, pp. 588–589. See also D. J. Macgowan, "Chinese Guilds or Chambers of Commerce and Trades Unions," *Journal of the Royal Asiatic Society, North China Branch,* August, 1886, pp. 133–192; and Hosea Ballou Morse, *The Gilds of China—with an Account of the Gild Merchant or Co-Hong of Canton* (Shanghai: Kelly and Walsh, 1932).

103. See A. W. Loomis, "The Six Chinese Companies," *Overland Monthly,* New Series 2 (September 1868): 221–227; William Speer, "Democracy of the Chinese," *Harper's Monthly* 37 (November 1868): 844–846; Richard Hay Drayton, "The Chinese Six Companies," *The Californian Illustrated Magazine* 4 (August 1893): 472–477; Fong Kum Ngon (Walter N. Fong), "The Chinese Six

Companies," *Overland Monthly,* May, 1894, pp. 519–526; Charles Frederick Holder, "The Dragon in America: Being An Account of the Workings of the Chinese Six Companies in America and its Population of the United States with Chinese," *The Arena* 32 (August 1904): 113–122; William Hoy, *The Chinese Six Companies* (San Francisco: Chinese Consolidated Benevolent Association, 1942); Tin-Yuke Char, "Immigrant Chinese Societies in Hawaii," *Sixty-First Annual Report of the Hawaiian Historical Society* (Honolulu: Advertiser Publishing Co., 1953), pp. 29–32; Chu Chai, "Administration of Law Among the Chinese in Chicago," *Journal of Criminal Law* 22 (March 1932): 806–818.

104. See Rose Hum Lee, *The Chinese in the United States of America, op. cit.,* pp. 147–161; Calvin Lee, *op. cit.,* pp. 34–35. In Canada, a crackdown on illegal immigration from Hong Kong and China led to a highly misleading article attacking the Chinese in racist innuendoes and accusing the Chinese Benevolent Association of complicity in the crimes. See Alan Phillips, "The Criminal Society that Dominates the Chinese in Canada," *Maclean's: Canada's National Magazine* 75 (April 7, 1962): 11, 42–44, and the letter from Stanford Lyman and William Willmott to the editor, *ibid.,* 75 (May 19, 1962): 6. Recently in San Francisco, disaffected immigrant Chinese youth and disenchanted American-born youth have formed separate associations and publicly rebuked the Chinese Six Companies for their insensitivity in Chinatown. See the San Francisco *Chronicle,* March 18, 19, 1968. News of this effort is regularly reported in *East-West,* a San Francisco journal published in Chinatown. For the community's social problems, see Stuart H. Cattel, *Health, Welfare, and Social Organization in Chinatown* (New York: Community Service Society, 1962), pp. 20–90.

105. The Six Companies aroused the ire of impoverished Chinese, a few missionaries, and an occasional sea captain for their ruthless and unstinting efforts to collect debts. See Otis Gibson, *The Chinese in America* (Cincinnatti: Hitchcock and Walden, 1877), pp. 339–344; Loomis, "The Six Chinese Companies," *op. cit.,* p. 223; testimony of Thomas H. King, *Report of the Joint Special Committee, op. cit.,* p. 95. It still collected debts from departing Chinese as late as 1942 and also required those returning to China to pay a departure fee. See Hoy, *op. cit.,* pp. 23–24.

106. In the following there is only a brief discussion of one of the most fascinating elements of overseas Chinese life. For a more complete discussion, see Stanford M. Lyman, "Chinese Secret Societies in the Occident: Notes and Suggestions for Research on the Sociology of Secrecy," *Canadian Review of Sociology and Anthropology* 1 (May 1964): 79–102.

107. Meadows, *op. cit.*, pp. 112–120. Sun Yat-sen's relations with secret societies are described in S. Y. Teng, "Dr. Sun Yat-sen and Chinese Secret Societies," in Robert Sakai, ed., *Studies on Asia, 1963* (Lincoln: University of Nebraska Press, 1963), pp. 81–99; Sun Yat Sen, *Memoirs of a Chinese Revolutionary: A Programme of National Reconstruction for China* (London: Hutchinson & Co., n.d.), pp. 184–224. See also James Cantlie and C. Sheridan Jones, *Sun Yat Sen and the Awakening of China* (New York: Fleming H. Revell, 1912), pp. 86–126; Stephen Chen and Robert Payne, *Sun Yat-sen: A Portrait* (New York: John Day, 1946), pp. 1–176; Marius B. Jansen, *The Japanese and Sun Yat-sen* (Cambridge: Harvard University Press, 1954), pp. 59–130; Shao Chuan Leng and Norman D. Palmer, *Sun Yat-sen and Communism* (London: Thames and Hudson, 1962), pp. 1–34; Paul Linebarger, *Sun Yat Sen and the Chinese Republic* (New York: Century, 1925), pp. 115–282; Mariano Ponce, *Sun Yat-sen: The Founder of the Republic of China* (Manila: Filipino-Chinese Cultural Foundation, 1965); Lyon Sharman, *Sun Yat-sen: His Life and its Meeting—A Critical Biography* (Hamden, Conn.: Archon, 1965), pp. 29, 61–64, 84–86, 97, 109, 113–114; Henry Bond Restarick, *Sun Yat Sen: Liberator of China* (New Haven: Yale University Press, 1931), pp. 11–108. Two post-1949 Chinese publications also speak of Dr. Sun's relations with secret societies: *Dr. Sun Yat-sen: Commemorative Articles and Speeches by Mao Tse-tung, Soong Ching Ling, Chou En-lai, and Others* (Peking: Foreign Languages Press, 1957), pp. 14–16, 70–72; Wu Yu-chang, *The Revolution of 1911: A Great Democratic Revolution of China* (Peking: Foreign Languages Press, 1962), pp. 16–30. For the communist suppression of secret societies, see A. Doak Barnett, *China on the Eve of Communist Takeover* (New York: Praeger, 1963), pp. 83, 91–92, 126–129; Theodore H. E. Chen, *Thought Reform of the Chinese Intellectuals* (Hong Kong: Hong Kong University Press, 1960), pp. 108–111.

108. In addition to Comber, *op. cit.*, see J. S. M. Ward and W. G. Stirling, *The Hung Society or the Society of Heaven and Earth*, 3 vols. (London: Baskerville Press, 1925–26); Mervyn Llewelyn Wynne, *Triad and Tabut: A Survey of the Origin and Diffusion of Chinese and Mohammedan Secret Societies in the Malay Peninsula, A. D. 1800–1935* (Singapore: Government Printing Office, 1941); J. M. Gullick, *The Story of Early Kuala Lumpur* (Singapore: Donald Moore, 1956); J. M. Gullick, *A History of Selangor, 1742–1957* (Singapore: Eastern Universities Press, 1960), pp. 41–90; Maurice Freedman, "Immigrants and Associations: Chinese in Nineteenth-Century Singapore," *Comparative Studies in Society and History* 3 (October 1960): 25–48; Song Ong Siang, *One Hundred Years' History of the Chinese in Singapore* (Singapore: University of Malaya Press, 1967); Chen Mock Hock, *The Early Chinese Newspapers of Singapore, 1881–1912* (Singapore: University of Malaya Press, 1967), pp. 46–47, 59–60, 82, 95–97, 119, 138–139.

109. Stanford M. Lyman, W. E. Willmott, and Berching Ho, "Rules of a Chinese Secret Society in British Columbia," *Bulletin of the School of Oriental and African Studies* 27, no. 3 (1964): 530–539.

110. See the three essays by Stewart Culin, "Chinese Secret Societies in the United States," *Journal of American Folk-Lore* 3 (January –March 1890): 39–43; "The I Hing or 'Patriotic Rising,' A Secret Society Among the Chinese in America," *Report of the Proceedings of the Numismatic and Antiquarian Society of Philadelphia for the Years 1887–1889*, November 3, 1887, pp. 51–59; "The Gambling Games of the Chinese in America," *Publications of the University of Pennsylvania; Series in Philology, Literature, and Archaeology* 1, no. 4 (1891): 1–17. For Dr. Sun's skepticism about the Chinese secret societies in America, see Sun Yat Sen, *op. cit.*, pp. 190–191, 215; for his skepticism about those in Malaya, see Chen Mock Hock, *op. cit.*, pp. 95–97n.

111. Alexander McLeod, *Pigtails and Gold Dust: A Panorama of Chinese Life in Early California* (Caldwell, Idaho: Caxton, 1947), pp. 149–150; Carl Glick, *Double Ten: Captain O'Banion's Story of the Chinese Revolution* (New York: Whittesley House, 1945); Restarick, *op. cit.*, p. 103.

112. Information on Seto May-tong is from *An Appeal for the Contri-*

bution of Essays Celebrating the Eighty-first Birthday of Mr. Seto May-tong and for Monetary Gifts Serving as the Foundation Fund of the May-tong Memorial School (1948), a document in Chinese presented to the author by a former member of the *Chih-kung T'ang.*

113. *Chung-Kuo Hung-Mun Ming-Tse Tang Declaration, Political Outline, and Constitution* (Shanghai, September, 1947); *The Declaration of Alliance of Middle Parties* (Shanghai and Nanking, February 21, 1948). These documents are in possession of the author.

114. See Lyman, "Chinese Secret Societies," *op. cit.,* pp. 99–100.

115. Calvin Lee, *op. cit.,* pp. 34–37.

116. Sixteenth Census of the United States, "Characteristics of the Non-White Population by Race," p. 7, "Race by Nativity and Sex for the United States, 1850–1940," p. 19; Seventeenth Census of the United States, "Non-white Population by Race," pp. 3B–19. See also Coolidge, *op. cit.,* p. 502.

117. United States Population Census, 1960, "Non-white Population by Race," *Final Report,* PC(2)-1C (Washington, D. C., 1963), p. 4.

118. Two settlements of Chinese—one in Trinidad in 1806–1814, the other in Hawaii in 1852—foundered because of the failure of Chinese women to join the men in the overseas venture. See Eric Williams, *History of the People of Trinidad and Tobago* (Port-of-Spain: PNM Publishing Co., 1962), p. 77, and Ralph S. Kuykendall, *The Hawaiian Kingdom: Foundation and Transformation, 1778–1854* (Honolulu: University of Hawaii Press, 1957), p. 329.

119. See Stanford M. Lyman, "Marriage and the Family Among Chinese Immigrants to America, 1850–1960," *Phylon Quarterly* 29 (Winter 1968): 321–330.

120. Freedman, *Lineage Organization, op. cit.,* pp. 19–20, 32, 101–105. There was much variation in practice. See Freedman, *Chinese Lineage and Society, op. cit.,* pp. 43–67. See also Wen Yen Tsao, "The Chinese Family from Customary Law to Positive Law," *Hastings Law Journal* 17 (May 1966): 727–765.

121. For a good fictional account, see James A. Michener, *Hawaii* (New York: Random House, 1959), pp. 399–401.

122. The remittances continued well into the twentieth century and were

a principal element of the Republican economy. See Arthur N. Young, *China and the Helping Hand, 1937–1945* (Cambridge: Harvard University Press, 1963), pp. 79, 178, 262–263. From July, 1937, to December, 1941, the Chinese Overseas Affairs Commission reported receipt of $61,985 from the United States. Chinese Ministry of Information, comp., *China Handbook, 1937–1943: A Comprehensive Survey of Major Developments in China in Six Years of War* (New York: Macmillan, 1943), p. 37.

123. See Siu, *op. cit.,* pp. 35–41. See also Paul C. P. Siu, "The Isolation of the Chinese Laundryman," in Ernest W. Burgess and Donald Bogue, *Contributions to Urban Sociology* (Chicago: University of Chicago Press, 1964), pp. 429–442.

124. A good example is found in a United States Government report: "The Chinese coolie seldom or never removes his wife or family from his original domicile. They are left to represent his home interest with his ancestral divinities. The women are still less inclined to travel than the men. Without any education or mental development, Chinese females cherish exaggerated terrors of the fierce 'outside barbarians,' and of the tempestuous seas. A number of high class females have arrived in this country, the wives of intelligent merchants and business men, whose belief in the popular creed is not more profound than that which the ancient philosophers cherished for the classic mythology; but of the laboring classes it is believed that not a single instance of this character has yet been reported . . . . It is evident, that with the Chinese female immigration already secured, no permanent family organization can be expected, and that consequently the Chinese race will not be propogated in this country. Their continuance as part of our population is then limited to the natural life of the immigrant." "Chinese Labor in Agriculture," *U. S. Department of Agriculture Reports,* 1870, pp. 573–574.

125. *Case of the Chinese Wife* 21 Fed. 785 (1884); Huang Tsen-ming, *op. cit.,* pp. 84–85.

126. Timothy J. Molloy, "A Century of Chinese Immigration: A Brief Review," *Monthly Review of the United States Immigration and Naturalization Service* 5 (December 1947): 69–75.

127. From a silver mining camp in Nevada in 1869 comes a terrible incident: "None were treated as beastly as the Chinese women from the brothels. One prostitute tried to run away from her owner and

hide in the hills, but she was finally captured and held prisoner. Living in the open, exposed to the elements during her brief period of freedom, she had frozen both feet. The flesh fell away from the bones before her master asked admission to the hospital for her and then both feet had to be amputated. Although the wounds healed rapidly, the patient courted death, refusing to take medicine or food. She was eventually returned to the home of her owner to pass into oblivion without a protest from society." W. Turrentine Jackson, *Treasure Hill: Portrait of a Silver Mining Camp* (Tucson: University of Arizona Press, 1963), p. 65.

128. Horace Greeley, "California Mines and Mining," Sacramento, August 7, 1859, *An Overland Journey: From New York to San Francisco in the Summer of 1859,* edited by Charles T. Duncan (New York: Knopf, 1964), pp. 245–246.

129. Henryk Sienkiwicz, *Portrait of America* (New York: Columbia University Press, 1959), p. 255.

130. A. W. Loomis, "Chinese Women in California," *Overland Monthly* 3 (April 1869): 344–351; Charles Frederick Holder, "Chinese Slavery in America," *North American Review* 165 (July 1897): 288–294; Louis J. Beck, *New York's Chinatown: An Historical Presentation of its People and Places* (New York: Bohemia Publishing Co., 1898), pp. 107–121; Carol Green Wilson, *Chinatown Quest: The Life Adventures of Donaldina Cameron* (Stanford: Stanford University Press, 1950).

131. The situation might have been mitigated if Chinese had been able to intermarry into the white population. In other areas of Chinese settlement, such as Indonesia, Chinese did intermarry. See Donald Earl Willmott, *The Chinese of Semarang: A Changing Minority Community in Indonesia* (Ithaca: Cornell University Press, 1960), pp. 103–116. However, in the United States, racial intermarriage had been illegal in thirty-nine states. In fourteen of these states, the law specifically prohibited marriage between Chinese or "Mongolians" and whites. California's anti-miscegenation statute was originally enacted in 1872 to prohibit marriage between Negroes or mulattos and whites; in 1906 it was amended to prohibit marriages between whites and "Mongolians." See Huang Tsen-ming, *op. cit.,* pp. 260–262; Fowler V. Harper and Jerome Skolnick, *Problems of the Family* (Indianapolis: Bobbs-Merrill, 1962), pp. 96–99; *Perez vs. Sharp* 32 Cal. 711, 2nd Ser. (1948); Andrew D.

Weinberger, "A Reappraisal of the Constitutionality of 'Miscegenation' Statutes," in Ashley Montagu, *Man's Most Dangerous Myth: The Fallacy of Race* (Cleveland: Meridian Books, World Publishing Co., 1964), pp. 402–424.

132. Remigio B. Ronquillo, "The Administration of Law Among the Chinese in Chicago," *Journal of Criminal Law* 25 (July 1934): 205–224.

133. Jacob A. Riis, *How the Other Half Lives: Studies Among the Tenements of New York* (New York: Sagamore Press, 1957), p. 76.

134. Frank Soulé, John H. Gihon, and James Nisbet, *The Annals of San Francisco* (Palo Alto: Lewis Osborne, 1966), pp. 411–412. Originally published in 1855.

135. Samuel Wells Williams, "The City of the Golden Gate," *Scribner's Monthly* 10 (July 1875): 272–273.

136. Soulé, Gihon, and Nisbet, *op. cit.,* pp. 378–379.

137. *California Senate Journal; Third Session,* 1852, pp. 168, 192, 205, 217.

138. "Minority Report of the Select Committee on Senate Bill No. 63 ...," *California Senate Journal; Third Session,* March 20, 1852, Appendix: 671.

139. Ping Chiu, *op. cit.,* pp. 89–128.

140. See James Bryce, "Kearneyism in California," *The American Commonwealth* (New York: Macmillan, 1901), 2: 425–488; Appendix: 878–880. See also Doyce B. Nunis, Jr., "The Demagogue and the Demographer: Correspondence of Denis Kearney and Lord Bryce," *Pacific Historical Review* 36 (August 1967): 269–288.

141. See Philip S. Foner, *Mark Twain: Social Critic* (New York: International Publishers, 1958), pp. 182–192.

142. Morton Keller, *The Art and Politics of Thomas Nast* (New York: Oxford University Press, 1968), pp. 217–242.

143. Philip S. Foner, *The Life and Writings of Frederick Douglass; Vol. IV: Reconstruction and After* (New York: International Publishers, 1955), pp. 46, 222, 262–266, 282, 339, 349, 352, 385, 440.

144. See Leon Litwack, *North of Slavery: The Negro in the Free States, 1790–1860* (Chicago: University of Chicago Press, 1965), pp. 167–168.

145. See Forrest G. Wood, *Black Scare: The Racist Response to Emancipation and Reconstruction* (Berkeley: University of California Press, 1968), pp. 97–101.

146. Bryce, *op. cit.*, 2: 880.

147. *The Workingmen's Party of San Francisco* (San Francisco: Bacon and Co., 1878). Quoted in N. Ray Gilmore and Gladys Gilmore, eds., *Readings in California History* (New York: Crowell, 1966), pp. 200–203.

148. Testimony of Frank M. Pixley in *Report of the Joint Special Committee, op. cit.*, p. 22.

149. Coolidge, *op. cit.*, p. 259.

150. C. P. Dorland, "Chinese Massacre at Los Angeles in 1871," *Annual Publication of the Historical Society of Southern California* (Los Angeles, 1894), pp. 22–26.

151. Coolidge, *op. cit.*, pp. 265–266; Oscar Lewis, *San Francisco: Mission to Metropolis* (Berkeley: Howell-North, 1966), pp. 136–139.

152. Ourada, *op. cit.*

153. P. B. Wilcox, "Anti-Chinese Riots in Washington," *Washington Historical Quarterly* 20 (July 1929): 204–212; Jules Alexander Karlin, "The Anti-Chinese Outbreaks in Seattle, 1885–1886," *Pacific Northwest Quarterly* 39 (April 1948): 103–130; Karlin, "The Anti-Chinese Outbreak in Tacoma, 1885," *Pacific Historical Review* 23 (August 1954): 271–283; Murray Morgan, *Skid Road: An Informal Portrait of Seattle* (New York: Viking, 1960), pp. 84–102.

154. Alan Morley, *Vancouver: From Milltown to Metropolis* (Vancouver: Mitchell Press, 1961), pp. 121–126.

155. Eliot Lord, *Comstock Mining and Miners* (Berkeley: Howell-North, 1959, originally published in 1883), pp. 355–359; Coolidge, *op. cit.*, pp. 254–277; Lewis, *op. cit.*, pp. 139–140; Vardis Fisher and Opal Laurel Holmes, *Gold Rushes and Mining Camps of the Early American West* (Caldwell, Idaho: Caxton Printers, 1968), pp. 262–265, 272–273.

156. *In re Tiburcio Parrot* 6 Sawyer 349 (1879); *In re Ah Chong* 6 Sawyer 451 (1880); *In re Lee Sing* 43 Fed. 359 (1890).

157. See *Soon Hing vs. Crowley* 113 U. S. 713 (1880); *People vs. Soon Kung,* unreported (1874); *People vs. Ex Parte Ashbury,* reported in *Daily Alta Californian,* February 5, 1871; *Yick Wo vs. Hopkins* 118 U. S. 356 (1885).

158. Fisher and Holmes, *op. cit.*, pp. 263–264; Rose Hum Lee, *The Chinese in the United States of America, op. cit.*, p. 267.

159. Coolidge, *op. cit.*, pp. 72–73; *Takahashi vs. Fish and Game Commission of California* 334 U. S. 410 (1947).

160. *Terrace vs. Thompson* 263 U. S. 197 (1923); *Porterfield vs. Webb* 263 U. S. 225 (1923); *Webb vs. O'Brien* 263 U. S. 313 (1923); *Frick vs. Webb* 263 U. S. 326 (1923); *Mott vs. Cline* 200 Cal. 434 (1927); *Morrison vs. California* 291 U. S. 82 (1934); *Oyama vs. California* 322 U. S. 633 (1927); *Sei Fuji vs. State of California* 242 P2nd 617 (1952).

161. See *Report of the Immigration Commission; Immigrants in Industry; Japanese and other Immigrant Races in the Pacific Coast and Rocky Mountain States,* United States Congress, Senate, 61st Congress, 2nd session, Senate Document 633, vol. 3 (Washington, D. C.: Government Printing Office, 1911), pp. 411–413.

162. *The Invalidity of the Queue Ordinance, op. cit.,* Appendix: 15–43; *Ho Ah Kow vs. Matthew Nunan* 5 Sawyer 552 (1879); Sandmeyer, *op. cit.,* pp. 54–55.

163. *People vs. Hall* 4 Cal. 399 (1854); *Speer vs. See Yup* 13 Cal. 43 (1855); *People vs. Elyea* 14 Cal. 144 (1855).

164. Quoted in William Warren Ferrier, *Ninety Years of Education in California, 1846–1936* (Berkeley: Sather Gate Book Shop, 1937), p. 98.

165. Ferrier, *op. cit.,* pp. 98–104; *Wong Hin vs. Callahan* 119 Fed. 381 (1902).

166. *Gong Lum vs. Rice* 275 U. S. 78 (1927).

167. See, for example, Cameron H. King, Jr., "Asiatic Exclusion," *International Socialist Review* 8 (May 1908): 661–669. A few exceptions to the general anti-Chinese sentiment of organized labor were found among the "radicals" who organized the International Workers of the World, the United Mine Workers of British Columbia, and the American Labor Union. The division among labor unions on "the Chinese question" is documented in Philip S. Foner, *History of the Labor Movement in the United States* (New York: International Publishers, 1957–1965), *Vol. I: From Colonial Times to the Founding of the American Republic,* pp. 425–428, 488–493; *Vol. II: From the Founding of the American Federation of Labor to the Emergence of American Imperialism,* pp. 58–60, 204–205; *Vol. III: The Policies and Practices of the American Federation of Labor, 1900–1909,* pp. 274–279, 426–429; *Vol. IV: The Industrial Workers of the World, 1905–1917,* pp. 81–82, 123–124.

168. Robert Seagar II, "Some Denominational Reactions to Chinese Immigration to California," *Pacific Historical Review,* February, 1959, pp. 49–66.

Chapter V: "Japanese-Americans: Some Costs of Group Achievement," by John Modell

References

1. Carey McWilliams, *Factories in the Fields: The Story of Migratory Farm Labor in California* (Boston: Little, Brown, 1939), p. 104.
2. Theodore Roosevelt to Kermit Roosevelt, February 4, 1907, quoted in Raymond A. Esthus, *Theodore Roosevelt and Japan* (Seattle: University of Washington Press, 1966), p. 149.
3. Lincoln Steffens, "California and the Japanese," *Colliers* 57 (March 25, 1916): 5.
4. Sidney G. P. Coryn, "The Japanese Problem in California," *Annals of the American Academy of Political and Social Science* 24 (September 1909): 48.
5. *Los Angeles Times,* April 20, 1913.
6. California State Federation of Labor, *Proceedings, 1904,* p. 47.
7. Henry Steele Commager, ed., *Documents in American History,* 6th ed. (New York: Appleton-Century-Crofts, 1958), 2: 225.
8. Letters to Hiram Johnson, April 5 and June 3, 1913, letters in Hiram Johnson Papers, Bancroft Library, University of California, Berkeley.
9. *Los Angeles Examiner,* October 17, 1920.
10. California State Board of Control, *California and the Oriental* (1920), p. 212.
11. California State Commission on Immigration and Housing, *Report of an Experiment Made in Los Angeles in the Summer of 1917 for the Americanization of Foreign-Born Women* (1917), p. 18.
12. Los Angeles Japanese Chamber of Commerce, Minutes, March 5, 1918. This unpublished document is in Archives of the Japanese American Research Project, University of California, Los Angeles.
13. "Letter of Warning from Sei Fujii," papers of the Survey of Race Relations on the Pacific Coast, major document 207, Hoover Institution, Stanford, California.
14. *Rafu Shimpo* (Los Angeles), English-language section, April 4, 1927.
15. Sakae Tsuboi, "The Japanese Language School Teacher," *Journal of Applied Sociology* 11 (1926–27): 163–164.

16. Daisuke Kitagawa, *Issei and Nisei, The Internment Years* (New York: The Seabury Press, 1967), p. 26.
17. *Rafu Shimpo,* English-language section, December 1, 1935.
18. Quoted in George Yasukochi, "A Study of the Vocational Experiences of University of California Alumni of Japanese Ancestry," mimeographed report for the National Youth Administration, 1941, pp. 2–3.
19. Jacobus ten Broek, Edward N. Barnhart, and Floyd W. Matson, *Prejudice, War and the Constitution* (Berkeley: University of California Press, 1954), pp. 99–208.
20. Letter, April 12, 1942, in Savage Papers, Department of Special Collections, University of California, Los Angeles.
21. Untitled mimeographed document, August 14, 1944, Los Angeles County Committee for Interracial Progress.
22. Quoted in United States Department of the Interior, War Agency Liquidation Unit, *People in Motion* (n.d.), p. 17.
23. Harry H. L. Kitano, *Japanese Americans: The Evolution of a Subculture* (Englewood Cliffs, N. J.: Prentice-Hall, 1969), p. 141.

Selected Bibliography

Beach, Walter G. *Oriental Crime in California.* Stanford: Stanford University Press, 1932.

Bloom, Leonard, and Reimer, Ruth. *Removal and Return.* Berkeley: University of California Press, 1949.

Broom. Leonard, and Kitsuse, John I. *The Managed Casualty.* Berkeley: University of California Press, 1956.

Daniels, Roger. *The Politics of Prejudice.* Berkeley: University of California Press, 1962.

Ichihashi, Yamato. *Japanese in the United States.* Stanford: Stanford University Press, 1932.

Kitano, Harry H. L. *Japanese Americans: The Evolution of a Subculture.* Englewood Cliffs, N. J.: Prentice-Hall, 1969.

Konvitz, Milton R. *The Alien and the Asiatic in American Law.* Ithaca: Cornell University Press, 1946.

McKenzie, R. D. *Oriental Exclusion.* Chicago: University of Chicago Press, 1928.

Millis, H. A. *The Japanese Problem in the United States.* New York: Macmillan, 1915.

Strong, Edward K., Jr. *Japanese in California.* Stanford: Stanford University Press, 1933.

ten Broek, Jacobus, Barnhart, Edward N., and Matson, Floyd W. *Prejudice, War and the Constitution.* Berkeley: University of California Press, 1954.

Thomas, Dorothy Swaine. *The Salvage.* Berkeley: University of California Press, 1946.

Chapter VI: "White Racism and Black Response in California History" by Velesta Jenkins

References
1. Delilah Beasley, *The Negro Trail Blazers* (Los Angeles: Mirror Printing, 1919), p. 60.
2. *Ibid.,* p. 60.
3. *Ibid.,* p. 61.
4. *Ibid.,* p. 177.

Additional Sources
Caughey, John W. *School Segregation on Our Doorstep.* Los Angeles: Quail Books, 1967.

Caughey, John W. *Segregation Blights Our Schools.* Los Angeles: Quail Books, 1966.

Forbes, Jack D. *Afro-Americans in the Far West.* Berkeley: Far West Laboratory for Educational Research and Development, 1966.

Frye, Hardy. "Negroes in Early California." *Southwestern Historical Quarterly,* February, 1967.

Lapp, Rudolph. "The Negro in Gold Rush California." *Journal of Negro History,* April, 1964.

Thurman, Sue Bailey. *Pioneers of Negro Origin in California.* San Francisco: Acme, 1949.

Chapter VII: "Conflict in the Fields: Mexican Workers in California Agri-Business" by Charles Wollenberg

References
1. Paul S. Taylor, *Mexican Labor in the United States,* 3 vols. (Berkeley: University of California Press, 1930–33), 1.

2. *Los Angeles Times,* May 10, 1928.
3. Brawley *News*, May 11, 1929.
4. Louis Bloch, "Report on the Strike of the Imperial Valley Cantaloupe Pickers," *Mexicans in California: Report of Governor C. C. Young's Mexican Fact-Finding Committee* (San Francisco: State Printing Office, 1930).
5. *Los Angeles Times,* May 9, 1928.

Additional Sources

Dunn, John Gregory. *Delano: The Story of the California Grape Strike.* New York: Farrar, Straus & Giroux, 1967.

El Malcriado. Delano. Newspaper of the United Farm Workers Organizing Committee.

Galarza, Ernesto. *Merchants of Labor: The Mexican Bracero Story.* San Jose: Rosicrucian Press, 1964.

Grebler, Leo. *Mexican Immigration to the United States: The Record and Its Implications.* Los Angeles: UCLA Mexican-American Study Project, 1965.

Griffith, Beatrice. *American Me.* Boston: Houghton Mifflin, 1948.

McWilliams, Carey. *Factories in the Fields: The Story of Migratory Farm Labor in California.* Boston: Little, Brown, 1939.

North From Mexico. New York: Monthly Review Press, 1961.

Samora, Julian, ed. *La Raza: Forgotten Americans.* Notre Dame: University of Notre Dame Press, 1966.

Chapter VIII: "Afro-Americans and Mexican-Americans: The Politics of Coalition" by Mervyn M. Dymally

Bibliography

Bryce, James. *The American Commonwealth.* New York: Macmillan, 1889.

Clark, Kenneth. *Dark Ghetto: Dilemmas of Social Power.* New York: Harper & Row, 1965.

Forbes, Jack D. *Afro-Americans in the Far West.* Berkeley: Far West Laboratory for Educational Research and Development, 1966.

Myrdal, Gunnar. *An American Dilemma: The Negro Problem and Modern Democracy.* New York: Harper & Row, 1962.

Schlesinger, Arthur M., Jr. *A Thousand Days: John F. Kennedy in the White House.* Boston: Houghton Mifflin, 1965.